Editor: I.C. van Hout

Beloved
Burden

How children are carried

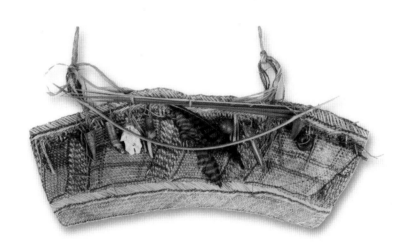

Tropenmuseum – Royal Tropical Institute
Amsterdam, the Netherlands

Beloved Burden – Baby-wearing around the world first appeared to accompany the exhibition Lieve Lasten in the Tropenmuseum in Amsterdam, 17 December 1993 – 28 August 1994.

The exhibition and this publication would not have been possible without the enthusiastic and positive support of an international group of experts. Rita Bolland and Attie Tabak made important contributions to the development of the idea of making cultural comparisons between the methods of carrying children. Various colleagues, from both within the Tropenmuseum and elsewhere, have played a critical and supportive role in the compilation of the book, in particular David van Duuren, Tony Lith and Hester Poppinga. In addition, we are grateful to the following museums for their cooperation: Rijksmuseum voor Volkenkunde, Leiden; Wereldmuseum, Rotterdam; Museon, The Hague; Ethnologisches Museum, Berlin; Museum of Mankind, London; Pitt Rivers Museum, Oxford; Musée de l'Homme, Paris; Musuem für Völkerkunde, Vienna; Russian Museum of Ethnography, St Petersburg; Museum of the American Indian, New York; Museum of Natural History, Washington. This publication was realised with the financial and practical support of the Tropenmuseum (part of the Royal Tropical Institute, Amsterdam) and the Nationale Commissie voor internationale samenwerking en Duurzame Ontwikkeling (NCDO) [National Commission for International Cooperation and Sustainable Development]. – *Itie van Hout, 1993*

Front cover photograph: Jannie Spruit-Engels, Studio Novum

Title page photograph: carry-cot from the Marind-Amim, Irian Jaya, made of strips of palm leaf and decorated with shells, teeth, feathers and a miniature bow with a bundle of arrows. This cot was used for a newborn boy. (Tropenmuseum collection)

This publication was realised with the suport of Kirsten Minnen, *forum voor Natuurlijk Ouderschap* (www.dragen-en-voeden.nl) and Karin Jeucken, *Little Shop around the Corner, voor moeder en kind natuurlijk* (www.littleshoparoundthecorner.nl).

Beloved Burden – Baby wearing around the world
Ed. I.C. van Hout – Amsterdam: Royal Tropical Institute

ISBN: 9789068321746

Keywords: baby slings / carry-cots / baby care; cultural anthropology / childcare; cultural anthropology

Unrefised reprint from the 1993 edition

Translation from Dutch: Steve Green

Final editing: Michael Blass

Original translations into Dutch: from Russian – Gertruud Alleman; from French – René de Graaff, Marieke Kehrer; from English – Wim Hart

Final editing of Dutch version: Geke van der Wal

Photos of objects: Fotobureau KIT, Irene de Groot / Paul Romijn

Drawings: Frans Stelling, after originals by the authors

Map: J. ter Haar, Hoofddorp, the Netherlands

Cover and graphic design: Grafisch ontwerpbureau Agaatsz, Meppel

Production: High Trade, Zwolle

Contents

How children are carried

I.C. van Hout

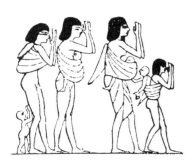

Egyptian wailing women carry their children at a funeral.
[Ploss, 1881]

In the West, increasing numbers of parents are carrying their newborn children in baby carriers. They prefer carrying their children on their bodies rather than transporting them in a pram or buggy. The advantages of this method of transporting babies are described in magazine articles. The novelty of this practice in the west is reflected in the lack of a single commonly accepted term for the object actually used for carrying the baby. Therefore, throughout this book the generic term 'baby carrier' will be used.

In regions where non-Western cultures prevail, it has been common practice for centuries to carry children in a variety of ways. Images dating from the time of the Pharaohs in Egypt prove that baby carriers were used long ago. Giotto's famous fourteenth century fresco in the Arena Chapel in Padua features Mary sitting on a donkey and carrying Jesus in a sling. There is evidence to suggest that the baby carrier was already used in the very earliest period of human history. It was perhaps one of the first implements ever made by humans.

Westerners have only recently discovered the advantages that this method offers. Nowadays, health experts point out that babies that are regularly carried in a baby carrier appear to be more content than those transported by pram. They cry less, thrive better and sleep more easily. Moreover, it facilitates breastfeeding. The constant proximity of parent and child can have a favourable effect on their relationship.

Not only human beings carry their offspring. Many animal species carry their young for varying lengths of time. It is one of the most striking phenomena relating to maternal behaviour among a wide variety of mammals. Why do they carry their newborn with them wherever they go? The reason probably lies in the composition of the mother's milk. Research has demonstrated that mammals whose milk is low in protein must feed their young frequently for prolonged periods, with only brief intervals. Mammals whose milk is protein-rich do the opposite. Rabbits, for example, feed their young only once, for four to five minutes, every twenty-four hours. The young can survive longer without their mothers. The mother's milk of primates, the species to which humans belong, has a low protein content, and their young must therefore be fed frequently. Feeding takes between ten and thirty minutes. For an infant to be fed regularly it must be carried. Young apes grip the fur on their mother's abdomen, often using the nipple as a fifth point of support; human infants require a baby carrier.

Humans have evolved without fur or the ability to grip very firmly, and so they had to create a means by which their young could be carried. It was impractical for a woman to carry her child in her arms, as she needed to have her hands free to carry out her daily tasks. Simple animal-skin or tree-bark baby carriers were therefore probably among the first expressions of human material culture.

There are also important social dimensions to the carrying of children. The child's primary experiences of the world come from the mother. Close to her, it gets to know its new environment. Following birth, the child continues to feel the rhythm of its mother's movements, and these form part of the child's perception of the world. Also the mother's scent, voice and warmth are comforting. The separation of a mother from her baby is not conducive to its development. Evidence of this was found as early as the twelfth century: an experiment was conducted at the behest of Frederick II, Holy Roman Emperor and King of Germany and Sicily. His chronicler, Alimbene, wrote 'He wished to discover which language and in what manner children would speak if they grew up never hearing anyone else speak.

The Flight to Egypt. Mary carries Jesus in a sling in front of her. Fresco by Giotto, c. 1306, in the Arena Chapel in Padua, Italy.
[See also page 58]

Inuit mother carries her child in an amauti.
[photograph Musée de l'Homme, Paris. See also page 132]

Women from White Russia at work with her child in a carry-cot on her back.
[Pokrowski, 1882]

Javanese woman with a child in a slendang.
[Ploss, 1881]

Native North-American Chinook woman carries her child in a carry-cot while fishing for salmon.
[Catlin, 1984]

He therefore ordered that a number of foster mothers and wet nurses only feed, bathe and clean the children in their care and not babble or talk with them. In this way he wished to discover which language they would speak: Hebrew, the most ancient language, Greek, Latin, Arabic, or most likely that of their biological parents. He never found out because all the children died. They could not stay alive without being lovingly spoken to or being cuddled and smiled at by their foster mothers.'

It is now generally accepted that a lack of contact and affection while growing up is detrimental to children. After carrying out research into several children's homes, the American child psychiatrist René A. Spitz came to the conclusion that small children who spend a lot of time alone and receive minimal attention from carers tend to lag behind in development. They exhibit restless, introverted behaviour. They do not learn to eat independently or become toilet-trained.

Just how important movement coupled with attention can be has been proven by research at the University of Louisiana in the United States of America. Two orphaned monkeys were brought up in separate cages, each containing an imitation mother. One made a rocking motion and the other remained im-mobile. After ten months, the monkey with the 'mother' that moved behaved normally, while the other was timid and anxious.

Paediatricians in Montreal claim that carrying children close to the body has a positive effect on their tendency to cry. Their research involves the comparison of two groups of mothers with children aged between four and twelve months. After several weeks it was found that children who had been carried more cried less. Experts agree that children who are frequently carried appear to be more content. They are alert and interested in their surroundings. When awake they observe the environment in which their mother is active. Their senses are stimulated because they have every opportunity to look, feel, smell, hear and taste.

Babies and small children are carried throughout the world, from Greenland to Tierra del Fuego, from Siberia to southern Africa and from Alaska to Australia. The way they are carried is influenced by climate. Living in temperatures as low as minus 30 degrees centigrade, no Inuit mother would place a child in a cradle because it would freeze to death. She carries her child on her back in the hood of her seal-fur coat, or *amauti*. Her body heat warms the child.

The baby carriers are made of materials found in the immediate area. Inhabitants of Canada and Siberia make carry-cots of birch bark lined with soft fur. Further south, where the climate is milder, wicker carrying baskets are used, often with a screen above the head to protect the child from the sun. In the tropics, mothers carry their children in slings made of light fabrics or straps.

A huge variety of cradles, baskets and straps are used for carrying. In regions where the winter is cool or cold – rather than extremely cold – and temperatures in the coldest months fall below 10 degrees centigrade, infants spend much of the day, and usually all of the night, in a carry-cot. In milder regions, children are normally carried for most of the day in a sling or strap. The child generally sleeps with its mother.

Children are carried in a variety of ways: on the back, abdomen or hip, or in clothing. There are many ways in which children can be carried on the back: using a forehead strap; with one band over one shoulder or two bands over two shoulders; in a cloth slung over one shoulder, under the other, and buttoned at the front; in a cloth draped over both shoulders and knotted in front; or one that passes under both arms and is also fastened at the front. If the child is carried on the hip, a carrying-strap or sling is employed. The child may also be carried in clothing with a large back, hood or pleat.

In most cultures where it is customary for children to be carried, babies lie in a carry-cot or are carried in a cloth bound to the body as soon as the mother resumes work. While she is busy the cot is usually hung in a tree or leant against something. Alternatively, a sling is used to bind the child to its mother's back while she is working. While the baby is still entirely dependent on its mother, she keeps it close to her. The amount of time spent in the cot or sling diminishes during the first year of life. An American researcher named Chisholm noted that between birth and the age of three months, babies spent an average of sixteen hours a day in the cot. By the child's first birthday this period had been reduced to only nine hours. As the child grows, and sometimes has to make way for a new baby, other people, usually grandmothers or older sisters, carry and take care of the child.

There are few statistics that tell us who carries the children, or over what sort of distances they are carried. One of the few investigations into this subject was made by Woodrow W. Denham, in the 1970s. He studied the carrying of children among the Alyawarra of Central Australia, a people who still live partly as hunter-gatherers. In 507 of the 510 cases observed, girls or women did the carrying; girls already start carrying smaller children from the age of five. It is notable that only the youngest baby is carried by the mother, in a wooden vessel on the hip. Slightly older toddlers

Anna Rupene and her daughter Huria, from the Hauraki district, New Zealand. Painted by Gottfried Lindauer in 1878.
[Pitt Rivers Museum, Oxford, UK]

Tibetan father with his daughter at the market.
[Photograph Herbert Paulzen]

are carried on the hip, shoulders or back. Most carrying takes place during trips to gather food, which are often lengthy.

In most cultures, the child accompanies its mother as she performs her daily tasks. During breaks, she takes the child on her lap or lays it beside her on the ground. People with a Western cultural background tend to do the reverse: the child is carried during leisure time, on the way to the day nursery or while shopping. Children are seldom carried while domestic chores are being done, and it is unheard of for a woman with a child in a sling to teach in a classroom or sit at a computer.

These differences in attitudes to carrying are reflected in the way children are cared for. In cultures where children are carried in a cradle for the first months of life, the custom of swaddling is also often encountered. But it is not only seen in these cultures: in the West too, newborn children were once tightly wrapped. Binding is a centuries-old tradition. The baby has a blanket, cloth or strap wound tightly or more loosely around it. Depictions of babies like this have been found on Byzantine mosaics from 1100 AD, in paintings from Pompeii and mediaeval frescoes by Giotto. The custom is common in regions with temperate climates and low humidity. The reasons given for binding babies vary according to culture. It is said that the child will become 'straight limbed', stay quieter, and be easier to trans-

port. In carry-cot cultures, and in a few sling cultures, small babies spend much of their time bound. As the child grows older, the periods it spends bound grow shorter and it is regularly given the opportunity to move freely. Studies have established that this practice need have no negative consequences for the child's development.

The second aspect of childcare that is closely linked with their being carried is toilet-training. This too is affected by climate. In warmer regions, where the child lies against the mother's body without a nappy, she will feel small restless movements when the child wishes to relieve itself. In cooler regions, a layer of dried moss or crushed cedar bark is placed in the carry-cot. This layer is replaced regularly so the child remains more or less dry. In Afghanistan, a hole is made in both the mattress and the cot. During swaddling a pipe is bound to the child's body so that bodily waste is led through a hole in the bottom of the cot. The pipe is round for a boy and oval for a girl.

This publication was produced to accompany the *Lieve Lasten* (Beloved Burden) exhibition at Amsterdam's *Tropenmuseum*. As the book was being compiled, it became clear that the child carrier is a perfect starting point to gain insight into the ways people care for their children in different cultures. Through focusing on the ways children are carried, many other aspects of culture – religious, social, economic, and pedagogical – come to light. They will be discussed further in the chapters that follow.

Although child carriers vary greatly, they share one characteristic: almost all are decorated to a greater or lesser degree. They are adorned with elaborate embroidery, appliqué or beading, in motifs with special significance. Amulets and attributes made of teeth, coins or beads are hung on the child carrier, which rattle when the mother walks: the decorated baby carrier is designed to protect the child both from earthly and supernatural misfortune.

There is a notable growth in the popularity of child carriers in Western (and Westernised) cultures. They evidently fulfil a need. More and more people are becoming convinced of their benefits. They are practical, and children thrive in them. And so the West is gradually incorporating an important element of non-Western cultures: the child carrier.

A traditionally dressed Japanese woman carries her child in a large fold in her kimono.
[Photograph World Arts Museum, Rotterdam]

Women on the road to the market in Banfora, Burkina Faso.

Part 1

A baby carrier in the form of a pomegranate, South China. The pomegranate, with its countless seeds, symbolizes wealth both in fertility and in material things.

[Property of Eric Boudot, Hong Kong]

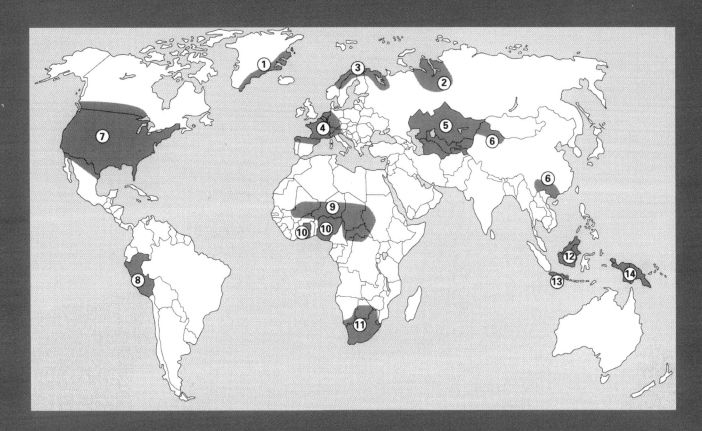

See part 2 and 3:

Chapter 1.1

The meaning of symbolic ornamentation

I.C. van Hout

In Western cultures, children spend a substantial part of the early phase of their lives in their cots. In non-Western cultures, the cot is almost unknown, and babies spend their first months in constant close physical contact with their mothers. During this period, the mother carries her child with her wherever she goes: on her back in a cloth or basket, on her hip in a sling, in a carry-cot hung from the shoulder, or in a net worn on the back and supported by a band around the forehead. In this way, care for the child is combined safely and practically with the execution of tasks such as working the land or preparing food.

The objects employed for carrying children vary from simple carrying-straps to baskets that are often decorated with a variety of symbols. There are many differences between the ways children are nursed and reared in differ-ent cultures. However, if we focus on the meaning of the objects created specially for the care and protection of children, there is a remarkable degree of correspondence between them. Almost all carry messages that relate to the health and welfare of the child. Portable baskets and cots are generally made to protect the newborn against physical harm, illness and malign supernatural forces, and to en-courage good health, good fortune and growth.

The Kenyah, who live in Borneo, construct carrying baskets notable for the ingenious beading that decorates them. Other signifi-cant objects are also hung from the basket: special coins, the teeth of certain animals or a snail shell containing the dried umbilical cord.

It is customary among the North American Arapaho to dry a newborn child's umbilical cord and keep it in a small, specially designed sack. This sack is lozenge-shaped and deco-rated with beads on two sides. It accompanies the child during the first few years of its life, attached to its carry-cot. Significant figures, motifs and colours are also applied to the cot itself. The motifs found on carry-cots are iden-tical to those found on Arapaho tents.

In southern China, slings in the form of a pomegranate are used on special occasions. These red cloths are decorated with embroi-dered motifs, copper sequins and glass beads. In the middle of the cloth is a round mirror.

These are just a few examples of the slings and portable baskets and cradles used in vari-ous parts of the world that are notable for their fine decoration and symbolic ornamen-tation. The care with which these objects are crafted, and the nature of the adornments, bear witness to great creativity and are all evi-dence of the correspondence mentioned earlier. These objects have exceptional significance for their users.

Why is so much attention in disparate cul-tures paid to the symbolic aspects of an imple-ment used for childcare? Why are they decorated with often complex motifs and hung with valuable amulets? Why are newborn children surrounded by symbols intended to promote their well-being?

Reproduction is elementary to the continuance of the human species. Children guarantee the survival of the community. Communities organise in various ways: some live in large extended families, and others in households with only the father, mother and children. But children are essential links in the chain of life whatever form this organisation takes. For this reason, having children has a religious significance in many societies. Children affirm bonds with the past, with ancestors and with the future – the coming generations that will perpetuate and shape the community. Factors such as these are essential constituents of many societies' cultures. Fertility is manifested in the bearing of children. Moreover, together with its associated rituals, fertility plays an extremely important role in the most disparate cultures. One of the manifestations of religious concepts relating to fertility and children – the tangible consequence of fertility – is the form that child-carriers take. In some regions, it is the material of which the carrier itself is made that is significant, while in others it is the decorations and amulets that have symbolic value.

That children are seen as links in a chain of life is apparent among the Pueblos in the southwest of the United States of America, for whom the carry-cot is a sacred object. It is carefully guarded and must always remain in the family's possession. The number of children who have been carried in it over the years is indicated by notches cut into its wooden frame. The Pueblos also believe that the disposal of the cot will cause the death of a child. Should a child die during the period that it is carried, the cot is burnt or placed in the grave – other peoples bury the child in its cot. The cot containing the dead child may alternatively be floated on a river, and allowed to be

An umbilical-cord amulet from North America. This type of amulet is often shaped as a lozenge or turtle, a symbol of longevity.
[Museum voor Volkenkunde (Ethnological Museum), Rotterdam]

borne away by the current to the land of its ancestors. North Australian aboriginals practise rites during which members of the group are connected to ancestors from Creation Time. One of the first they participate in is the 'smoke ceremony', which is performed by a newborn child's mother and grandmother to protect it from ill-health. Branches from the conkerberry bush, together with dampened bark and green leaves, are placed in a shallow fire pit and set alight. A dense smoke rises. The mother gives the *pitchi*, or carry-cot, containing the child, to the grandmother. She then sprinkles some milk from her breasts onto the

Fali woman from Cameroon. This animal-hide carrier is decorated with sorghum grass and cowry shells.
[Foto Angela Fisher, 1985]

made have a symbolic meaning. This occurs in Africa and elsewhere. In Cameroon and Senegal, mothers carry their children in sacks made of animal skins to which beads and cowrie shells are attached as ornaments. It is not by chance that these particular shells are chosen to decorate the sacks; they closely resemble the external female genitalia. Various peoples consider them to be symbols of fertility that may prevent sterility in women and protect small children from disease. They also offer protection against wizardry and malign spirits.

The pomegranate-shaped slings from southern China described above are apparently symbols of abundance. Because of the many seeds it contains, the pomegranate represents material wealth and fecundity. The embroidery work on the slings depicts animals, flowers, insects and mythical creatures such as the phoenix and the dragon. Birds are rendered with the Chinese sign for 'a long life'. Small bells keep demons at bay. Should an evil spirit nonetheless dare to venture near, it will be frightened off by its reflection in the round mirror at the centre of the sling. It will beat a hasty retreat and the child's soul will be safe.

The lozenge shape has a particular meaning for the North American Arapaho. It symbolises the navel, mankind, and a life of plenty. A newborn child's umbilical cord is placed in a lozenge-shaped bag and attached to the carrycot. This represents the child's origins, what it will become and what is wished for it. The application of identical motifs on both tent and cot expresses the wish that the baby will prosper and grow, and reach the age at which it can live independently in a tent of its own. The colours of the decorations – red, black and white – are also significant: red stands for blood and life, black for the hair colour of the young, and white from the hair colour of the elderly. The amulet, the symbols and the colours on a carry-cot provide the young life with protection against all manner of dangers.

fire, and the grandmother sways the child through the purifying smoke. In this way, the child begins its life with the three-fold blessing of the Earth Mother and the tribe mothers: conkerberry fire and smoke, mother's milk and grandmother's unwavering hand.

Hmong mothers in northern Thailand start making a sling immediately after the birth of a daughter. The newborn child is not carried in it herself, but when she grows up and has children herself, she is given it to carry her own children. Thus, for the first part of her life she is carried in a sling made by her grandmother. The sling is therefore a symbolic expression of the succession of generations.

As mentioned earlier, in some cultures the materials from which the child carriers are

It is not always the motifs or materials used that suggest a connection with fertility. For example, all textiles among the Colombian Ika people are made by men, and the weaving process itself is seen as analogous to the development of the placenta. Weaving thus promotes fertility.

Decorations on baby carriers frequently reflect the manner in which people experience their environment, their reality. Powers are attributed to these decorations and certain objects, motifs and materials that protect their users from undesirable external forces.

When a child is born, the parents, family or community hope that the child will grow and flourish. However, the child's chances of survival depend largely on the region and culture into which it is born. The period following birth is a tense one for the child and its parents: biologically, because the newborn child is so vulnerable, and culturally, because it must be accepted by the community as a whole.

Children often die of illnesses and phenomena that are attributed by the culture concerned to the activities of supernatural forces: gods, demons and ancestral spirits. Furthermore, the natural environment, the most important source of food, is often considered dangerous. Locals tend to avoid hazardous places in mountains and gorges, as well as certain stream and path crossings. In some agrarian societies too, nature is considered an indomitable phenomenon. Although it provides life's necessities, it also brings disasters such as failed harvests and cattle disease, which ensures a high level of insecurity.

Another source of danger is found at the level of interpersonal relationships. People and other beings may cause disease and misfortune. Attempts are made to ward off impending calamity caused by these beings, forces and spirits by appeasing them with gifts or sacrifices. Alternatively it is possible to resort to incantations or threats of violence reprisal.

In an effort to explain the extreme vulnerability of young children, societies often develop particular ways of thinking. Various peoples, for example the Kenyah Dayak of Central Kalimantan, believe that the soul of the newborn child is not yet fully bound to its earthly frame. If the soul removes itself, the consequences for the child can be fatal. Illness and death may result. To avert this the Dayak attach protecting amulets to their baby carriers. Thus the carrier contributes to the welfare of the child in a number of ways. Much attention is paid to the decoration of the basket: the underlying belief is that the basket should be made as attractive as possible, so that the soul will want to stay nearby. In addition, amulets, such as the previously mentioned snail shells containing the dried umbilical cord of the infant, special coins, and the teeth of certain animals, are attached to the basket. These make a rattling sound when the mother walks. This keeps the evil spirits, who want to lure away the soul of the child, at a distance.

The Maya of Guatemala, as well as other peoples of Central and South America, also wrap and carry the newborn child in a sling. This not only protects the infant from the sun, the cold overnight, and rain, but also ensures that the soul of the infant is not lost. They

Native North American Arapaho decorate the tops of their baby carriers with this type of motif.
[Kroeber, 1979]

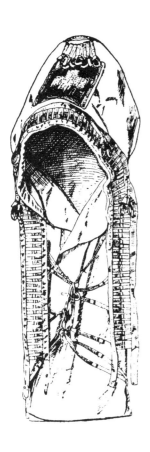

Arapaho baby carriers. They feature symbols that are also applied to tents. The symbols express the wish that the child will flourish in the carrier.
[Kroeber, 1979]

believe that when the soul leaves the body, the way is clear for witches or evil spirits that can cause illness or even the death of the infant. The soul of the newborn baby is especially vulnerable and may want to leave the body if it receives a major trauma. The sling, in which the child is hardly visible, protects the child and conceals it from the eyes of demons and evil spirits.

Many peoples have developed religious images that express man's dependence on the environment in an effort to cope with such uncertainties and fears. They therefore believe in the existence of mountain gods, and the image of Mother Nature is an everyday reality. Through these religious images, people orientate themselves to life and the world that surrounds them. Especially in uncertain and dangerous situations, these religious images play an important role. Events such as illness and death bring up many questions: people are confronted with the fact of finite human existence in a world that is largely unknowable and uncontrollable. In these situations, they seek ways of reducing their feelings of uncertainty, and find solace in certain forms of religious ceremonies and magical rituals.

In these societies, illness is often the harbinger of death. In particular, babies and children die, because they are more vulnerable. Illness is seen as the disturbance of the relationship between man and his surroundings. To redress this disturbed relationship, people engage in rituals they believe will have an appeasing effect on the supernatural powers that have manifested themselves undesirably.

The anthropologist, Spier, describes the rituals performed by a local healer in the Peruvian part of the Andes to cure a sick girl. The healer sat with the child at a table, on which a multicoloured infant's sling had been laid. He wound red wool around his index finger to ward off evil spirits. He then read the past and future from coca leaves scattered on the sling. He inspected the sacrifice to be offered to Mother Earth and wrapped it in the sling. He examined the girl by passing a multicoloured stone over her body. In this way the healer removed the illness. Subsequently the child was wrapped in the sling. After the right place for the sacrifice had been ascertained, it was offered to Mother Earth.

In this healing ritual, the sling in which the child was carried during the first years of her life had a special function. The illness is seen as a disturbance in the relationship between the child and her surroundings. To restore the relationship a sacrifice is made to Mother Earth. In leaving the sacrifice on the sling for some time and subsequently wrapping the child in it, the sling is used as an intermediary between the sick girl and her surroundings.

Religious rituals marking certain transitional faces in the life of an individual are an important aspect of community life. For example, the transition to adulthood, the celebration of a marriage, the birth of a child or the death of a member of the group. Transitions are really about uncertainty and commotion in both the community and the individual. They have a significance that surpasses the individual: they are also of significance for the community. This may be a threat to its more or less stable existence. To cope with uncertainties, religious ceremonies are transformed into concrete actions with social consequences. These rituals, which we call 'rites of passage', are performed with a certain societal objective. This objective may be vague and general, or it may be specific. The princi-

pal function of ceremonial and ritual acts is the promotion of continuity in the community. They reduce the possibly dangerous effects of regularly occurring changes. Different transitions are marked by different rituals.

Pregnancy celebrations and birth festivities are examples of transitional rituals. Rituals performed for the mother and the newborn child entail a large number of acts which 'soften' the birth and are intended to protect the mother and child (and sometimes also the father and the rest of the family) from unknown

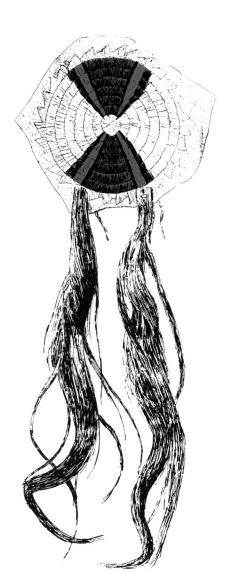

Native North American Arapaho tent decoration. The dark triangles are red. They symbolise tents in which the inhabitants are present. Red is the colour of life.
[Kroeber, 1979]

*Two carry cots. Porcupine
needles have been placed in the
North American Sioux carrier on
the right; the child has died.*
[Catlin, 1984]

dangers and the influence of evil. Certain ceremonies are held during the first ritual bathing of the mother and child, and when the remains of the umbilical cord drop off (as noted, these are often wrapped in a cloth or placed in a snail shell, which is then attached to the baby carrier) or when the child's hair is cut for the first time. These rituals serve to moderate the sometimes abrupt transitions from one life-phase to the next. People are thus given time to become accustomed to the new situation.

The indigenous Cayapo of the Brazilian Amazon consider the nurture of the newborn child to be an external phase of pregnancy. After birth, the infant is constantly carried in a sling by the mother. The child's hair may not be cut during this time. The child is considered to be a biologically and socially independent being only when it is no longer breastfed, at which time it can be admitted to the community. The Cayapo see this as symbolic of the child's parting from the mother. The cutting of the child's hair heralds the end of the period in which the child is transported by the mother in a sling. In Rwanda, in Africa, the period in which the child is carried by the mother is also considered a temporary prolongation of the union of mother and child. In some regions, women carry their babies on their backs in sheepskins specifically adapted for the purpose. The word used for the sheepskins is the same as that for placenta. This expresses the relationship between the placenta and the baby carrier, the dwelling of the child after birth. These peoples see the placenta both as an opening to and a protection against the violent outside world. Use of the carrier keeps the child near the mother, protected from the outside world, even after the actual birth has taken place. This softens the abrupt transition to life after birth.

Birth is not the only abrupt transition. The death of a child also heralds a sudden change. Under such circumstances, rituals that absorb the shock after the break in continuity are also performed. In such instances, a Cree mother in North America will carry the cradle board on her back for some time after her child has died. During this period of mourning the baby carrier is filled with straw. In this way she eases the sudden parting from her child.

The clinging baby monkey

Chapter 1.2

Animal carriers

D.A.P. van Duuren

Not all animals care for their offspring after birth. Motherly care is totally absent among sea turtles, for example. The female turtle struggles from the water, deposits her eggs in a shallow pit in the sand, covers them and returns to the sea. On hatching, the young turtles launch themselves into the surf. But without parental protection many fall prey to greedy predators. For this reason, few turtles reach adulthood.

Many other species of animal do care for and protect their young – some very actively. For a considerable period they may be occupied by feeding, cleaning, warming and training their progeny. Carrying and transporting the young is integral to protective behaviour.

This behaviour is not restricted to mammals; it is frequently observed among the lower orders of the animal kingdom. Wolf spiders, for example, carry a tangled mass of young on their backs. A similar phenomenon is observed among scorpions. Following birth, the young climb along the mother's protruding jaw to her back where they attach themselves as best they can by biting. Crocodile mothers sometimes transport their young in the space in their lower jaw, and some fish distend their mouths to create a tunnel into which their young can flee from approaching danger. Some water birds carry their chicks between folded wings on their back, perhaps protecting them from water rats and certainly allowing them to swim faster.

The higher the species, the stronger and more prolonged the bond between mother and young. For mammals this bond is a constant factor. The food the mother produces in her own body, milk, is an evolutionary innovation of the highest order. It inevitably creates a strong bond between older and younger generations.

The strength of the bond, and the manner in which the mother and her young relate, is intrinsically bound up with other aspects of the behaviour of the species. Mammals and birds can be divided into two categories: nest-fleeing (precocial) and nest-dwelling (nidicolous) species. Nest-fleeing animals leave the nest – if there is one – immediately after birth. Herding animals such as buffalo, horses and deer are born 'ready-made' as it were. Calves and foals walk unsteadily next to their mothers along with the group. Young hares too must immediately quit their nest, an open hollow in the ground. Nest-dwelling animals on the other hand are incomplete at birth. Their senses hardly function, if at all. They are blind, deaf, hairless and above all helpless in their nest or hole. It is essential that the mothers care for these young. For this reason, the young only of nest-dwelling species are carried. Mammals carry their young in a variety of ways: by biting the scruff of the neck, as many felines and some rodents do; with the entire head in the mouth, as the female bear does with her young; or on or under the body, as with sea otters, sloths and some anteaters. The best known of all carriers are the Australian marsupials. The miniscule and fur-less newborn kangaroo crawls to the nipples in its mothers pouch. Here it can develop and grow in a comfortable environment. The young koala bear even climbs onto its mothers back after leaving the pouch and is carried in this way for several months longer.

The young of more highly developed and intelligent mammals, for example the apes, are carried by, or attach themselves to, their mothers. For newborn animals of these species, the mother's body is a warm and furry nest – and a walking food supply. Temporary separation of the parent and child need not occur as it does among the nest-dwellers. In the early period of its existence the young ape and its mother form what resembles a single organism, an indivisible duality. The young one hangs – belly to belly – against its mother, using its hands and feet to grip her fur. It uses a nipple as a fifth point of support, although it does not drink continuously. This firm grip is necessary because usually the mother does not support the child. The infant ape is able to clamber over its mother's belly to a nipple. Even when sleeping, its grip adapts to changes in its mother's motion. Baby anthropoids spend the early part of their lives in close physical contact with the mother. Quite soon after birth, chimpanzees and gorillas are able to grip their mother's fur. For the first few days of life a baby gorilla has a hard time hanging on, but thereafter it is able to hold on almost entirely independently. Especially during the early phase, however, the mother often pro-vides support. She will change the baby's posi-tion herself or support it with an arm or upper leg if she feels the grip weakening or she needs to move quickly. Later on, when the child is heavier and more agile, the mother continues to carry it on her back.

[Photograph Artis Zoo, Amsterdam]

The core drive for this behaviour in mother-dependant species is the primary need for safety, warmth and protection. For this reason there is permanent physical contact between mother and offspring. Separation from the mother's body causes her young to become extremely fearful, as has been demonstrated by experiments with surrogate mothers: per-manent psychological damage can result.

Along with the ape and the anthropoid, humans belong to the primates. We can therefore assume that the bond between human mothers and their offspring is essentially similar in nature to those of apes. In other words, human children are also mother-dependent. There is, however, something remarkable and unique about human children. Primates are the most developed mammals: they all have large brains and a long life-expectancy, they suckle for a long time, they bear very few children at a time, and they are all well developed dexterous beings – all except human babies that is.

At the beginning of the twentieth century, when comparative studies of the anatomy and physiology of primates were providing hard evidence for the existence of biological evolution, L. Bolk, an anatomist from Amsterdam, the Netherlands, made a somewhat shocking pronouncement: he called humankind 'a retarded ape'. He based his conclusion on his comparisons of a human and a chimpanzee foetus. He observed that the physical characteristics of an ape change during its development after birth. For example, the hair on the head of a chimpanzee foetus later extends to cover its whole body and the initially prominent external reproductive organs have all but disappeared when the animal reaches adulthood. Foetal characteristics are, however, preserved in human infants. Head hair does not

Macaque with young.
[Photograph Artis Zoo, Amsterdam]

extend further, the stiff feet never gain the ability to grip, the flat nails do not become claws and the lowest vertebra do not become a tail. Bolk was of the opinion that the human child is no more than a matured embryo. It is unable to act independently. It is almost as helpless as the hairless pink newborn mouse that must be carried by the scruff of the neck by its mother.

But why? Why does most advanced primate, the human, produce offspring that is less developed than that of an ape? Why is this mother-dependant progeny unable even to cling to its mother? The answer to this question is surely to be found by investigating that which distinguishes humans: our brains and culture. Even after birth, humans do not develop quickly: prenatal retardation continues postnatally. When compared with those of other animals, the development of human motor function and physical maturation is akin to a film shown in slow motion. Everything takes longer for human child. For this reason, separation of mother and child also takes place later.

The unique character of the growth curve of the human brain plays a crucial role in this process. Most animals come into the world with completely, or almost completely, developed brains. This is not the case for humans: our brain-size increases fourfold during maturation. According to the American biologist S. J. Gould the reason for this is that birth itself, in any case a physical ordeal, would be impossible if the brains, and therefore the head, were fully grown. This explains the embryonic child with an enormous potential for learning.

For that is the essence of the 'naked ape' with large brains: its ability to learn during a slow and long, but nonetheless receptive, youth. Primates may win out in terms of biological evolution, but humans always come out on top due to their superior creative intellect. Not so much a naked ape, but a rational ape. Human nature is culture. But the human being remains a mother-dependent primate. The mothers have no fur and the children have no strong arms or gripping hands any more. The brains led the way.

The artificial baby carrier must have been developed as a direct result of the loss of the ability to carry safely by natural means. Early humankind's struggle for existence was hard. To remain alive was the priority. A great deal of the day was taken up searching for food, keeping warm, finding shelter and protecting children.

Small groups of hunter-gatherers were forced to roam the land. The materials and tools available to them were extremely limited: clubs and rocks as implements and weapons, and, undoubtedly, crude provision for the transportation of infants if the groups were roving or journeying great distances. Child carriers were in all probability made from animal hides or constructed from materials obtained from vegetation. Although we are uncertain as to their exact form, we can reasonably assume that child carriers belonged to the earliest products of material culture. In this context, the child carrier may be seen as one of the many bridges between nature and culture.

Comparative study on infant crying

Chapter 1.3

Crying and carrying

R.G. Barr

One of the mysteries about early behaviour is why infants cry so much in the first three months of life – more than at any other time in their lives. Furthermore, this crying is not just a random behaviour, but occurs in a predictable pattern. In general, the amount of crying that infants do tends to increase in the first two months of life, and then decrease in the third and four months. The crying also tends to cluster during the evening hours. While these *patterns* of crying hold true for most infants, the actual *amount* of crying by one infant can vary substantially from that of another. In many Western societies, infants who cry a lot are referred to as 'colicky'. Their crying is so severe and of such concern to parents that many of them are taken to physicians to determine whether they are sick or in pain.

One of the most common techniques used throughout human history to calm distressed infants is carrying and holding. Of course, carrying has other functions too: it permits the parent and infant to be close together while the parent is working, reduces the time of response to infants signals, and is part of the feeding act. These functions are facilitated by the use of carriers and slings that vary widely from culture to culture. Consequently, the reduction of infant distress for which carrying might be responsible is usually accomplished in the context of a 'caregiving package' that includes closeness of the parent and the infant, feeding frequency and responsiveness to infant signals. Interestingly, some of the more obvious changes in the recent history of human caregiving styles have been the extent to which carrying, feeding frequency, and frequency of parent responses have been reduced, especially in Western industrialised societies. For example the !Kung San hunter–gatherers of Botswana tend to carry their infants in a *kaross*, or sling, throughout the day. They feed their infants three to four times each hour, and seldom fail to respond to the shortest infant signals. By contrast, Western parents tend to carry their infants for about three hours per day, feed every two to four hours, and often do not respond to infant signals – sometimes for fear of 'spoiling' the child. Such differences in the caregiving package have understandably raised questions in the minds of parents and clinicians as to whether these changes affect the way infants behave. Similarly, they have provided scientists of human behaviour with an important tool with which to understand the determinants of behaviours such as crying, especially in the early post-newborn period, when crying is at its peak.

We have had the opportunity to carry out three studies that contribute directly to our understanding of the role of carrying in infant crying behaviour in natural settings. In the first, we compare the pattern, and duration and frequency of crying in !Kung San infants and Dutch and American infants. Because of the differences in caregiving practice, we expected that there would be differences in crying behaviour, but we were not certain of what those differences would be. The results showed convincingly that the duration of crying in the !Kung San was only about half as long as the Western infants. Interestingly, however, most of the pattern and the frequency of crying was the same in both groups. Both the differences and similarities are important. The reduction in crying duration in the absence of changing frequency means that the caregiving differences primarily seem to affect the length of crying bouts rather than how often infants cry. The fact that the early peak of crying occurs despite the wider differences in caregiving styles suggests that this aspect of crying is resistant to caregiving differences, and that it may be a universal characteristic of the human species.

In a second study, we asked specifically whether one of the salient differences between !Kung San and Western caregiving – carrying and holding – might be an important determinant of crying. In this study of Canadian mothers and infants, one group of mothers increased the amount of time spent carrying their babies between the fourth and twelve weeks of life to 4.4 hours per day on average. Another group carried their infants for 2.7 hours per day. The effects were quite striking. At six weeks of age, when the amount of crying is at its peak, the babies in the first group cried 1.2 hours per day compared to 2.2 hours in the second group – a 43 percent difference. When only early evening crying (between 4 pm and midnight) was considered, the first group cried 54 percent less than the second. However, as in the cross-cultural study, only the duration of crying was affected; the frequency of crying was the same for both

groups. This study provided impressive convergent evidence that caregiving differences are determinants of crying behaviour, but that they specifically seem to affect bout duration rather than frequency.

In a third study, we asked whether increasing carrying and holding on the part of caregivers might be useful as a therapy for infants who were presented to physicians by their parents with the complaint of 'colic' or excessive crying. Infants with colic have been notoriously resistant to almost all therapeutic manoeuvres, and are difficult problems for both parents and clinicians. If the findings in normal infants could be extended to infants with colic, then carrying might provide an easily accessible form of treatment. Half of the parents who brought their infants to the physician with this complaint were given advice about colic *and* asked to increase the amount of carrying they did by 50 percent.

The child sleeps as the mother prepares food. Hausa, Anka, northern Nigeria.
[Photograph B. Menzel 1961]

The other parents were given only the advice. It was impressive to note that these parents were already carrying their infants over four hours a day, even before the 'treatment' started. However, the additional carrying was not effective in reducing crying further. As is typical of infants with colic, the amount of crying slowly declined over the next few weeks, but this resolution of crying did not occur any faster because of carrying differences. Unfortunately, from the clinical point of view, this study did not give any encouragement that colic could be treated simply by increasing carrying. However, it did provide objective evidence that whatever causes these infants to cry seems to be resistant to change by soothing measures which are effective in infants without colic.

These carrying studies have provided significant insight into the determinants of this salient and important early infant behaviour. The distress-reducing function of carrying has been confirmed. They have also suggested that the presence of distress signals may have an important function for early survival, since neither the frequency not the pattern of crying are easily changed despite quite radical differences in caregiving practice.

What the studies do not demonstrate is whether or not we should carry our infants more. Decisions about infant care are made in the light of many biological and cultural considerations, of which the desire to have quiet babies is only one. However, it is clear that there is a wide range of choices within the human experience as to how, and how much, infants are carried. When these choices are made, some aspects of infant behaviour may be affected, but other aspects may not.

Premature babies in the pouch

Chapter 1.4

The kangaroo method

R. de Leeuw

With the kangaroo method, premature babies are removed from their incubators for periods and brought into close, skin-to-skin, contact with their parents – comparable to a young kangaroo's contact with its mother. This provides the child with a pleasant alternative to the incubator, and the parents with the opportunity to cherish their child. The method was first used in 1979 at the *Instituto Materno Infantil*, a maternity and perinatal hospital in the Colombian capital, Bogotá. It was later introduced elsewhere, including the Amsterdam teaching hospital, the AMC, in 1985.

The paediatricians Edgar Rey and Héctor Martínez Gómez began the *Programa Madre Canguro* (Kangaroo Mother Programme) in 1979 in Bogotá with the support of UNICEF. The underlying reason for setting up this project was that the conditions in the hospital for premature babies were wretched: several babies would lie together in a single incubator, leading to a greater susceptibility to hospital infections and an extremely high death rate. The hospital's policy towards the mothers was also pitiful. They were rarely permitted access to their children. They could not breastfeed despite this being very important to these mostly poor people. Frequently, even if it survived, the child was not collected by its mother.

In the *Programa Madre Canguro*, babies born prematurely are discharged from hospital after a period of stabilisation lasting a few days. They are placed, naked, against the mother's chest in the *posición canguro*. It is preferred that the children remain with their mother in this way for the ensuing weeks. They are intensively supported during this period by a programme of aftercare in a specialised outpatient department, *la casita*. *Amor*, *calor* and *lactancia maternal* (love, warmth and mother's milk) are central to this project. And although the project is beset with a number of problems, the prospects for premature babies born at the hospital are vastly improved.

One aspect of the programme, close physical contact, was adopted by a well-equipped ward of a modern hospital in a Western country.

Premature babies are underdeveloped and vulnerable and this makes it more difficult than normal for the child to adapt to the world outside its mother. It will often suffer problems associated with breathing, body-temperature regulation, feeding and infection. It must therefore be admitted to an incubator ward and receive special care. Very premature, very small, and sickly premature children are even admitted to a special intensive care ward for newborns.

Developments in medical techniques and the growth of experience in the care sector for these children have led to an enormous improvement in the prospects for babies born extremely early – in developed countries in any case. Nowadays, even children born 13 or 14 weeks early with a birth weight between 500g and 1000g can survive. However, survival is not guaranteed. Many very premature babies die, and some that survive are handicapped.

There are also psychosocial problems regarding premature children. When a child is born too early, preparations for parenthood, and the pregnancy itself, are not yet complete. The child must be admitted to hospital, is in danger, and must be treated by specialists using complex equipment, all of which contributes to creating a high level of anxiety. There may be feelings of disappointment and especially fear - fear for the baby's life or fear of a possibly imperfect future. Furthermore, feelings of guilt play a role. Parents feel that they have failed. Their child is lying in an incubator, at a distance; they can do nothing to help it, and initially they may not dare to. Others take care of their child – the parents are not allowed to – themselves, and they must simply await the outcome. Until the late 1970s, contact between parents and children in this situation was greatly hindered. They were not even permitted to see their children from nearby, let alone make physical contact. This often seriously disturbed the development of parent-child relationships.

Fortunately, changes began to take place in the 1980s. Parents became welcome 'guests' on the incubator ward and they were permitted increasing levels of contact: touching, taking the child onto the lap and assisting in its general care. The breakthrough came in 1985, however, when the incubator ward of the *Academisch Medisch Centrum* in Amsterdam adopted the kangaroo method. It involves the baby being removed from the incubator and being held, in a more or less vertical position, against the mother or father's chest. It is then covered up with a blanket. In almost all cases, this is done once or twice a day for an hour or more. Babies seem to enjoy it, and generally benefit from it. The method was gradually entirely integrated into the care of babies and parents. Its practice has drawn exceptionally positive reactions from parents, doctors and nursing staff.

The nurse responsible for each baby determines whether the kangaroo method is appropriate or not. The deciding factors are the stability of the child's breathing pattern and of its circulation. If necessary, these functions can continue to be monitored. Temperature is generally not an issue. The room in which it takes place is warm (26 to 27°C), the child lies against the parent's chest and is covered. As long as care is taken, the drip forms no real obstruction. If the child needs extra oxygen, this can be provided by placing a mask near its face. Due to improved breathing while in this position, however, the premature baby's need for extra oxygen diminishes.

Premature babies have an increased susceptibility to infections, but this rarely causes problems in relation to the kangaroo method. Parents do receive pointers on general hygiene and are advised to shower daily. Research into the efficacy of the method for very premature children, whose health was not yet stabilised, found it to be very safe. Breathing, blood circulation, body temperature and behaviour were not negatively affected.

While the child is in this position, it can have many new experiences. It makes eye contact, it investigates the nipples or chest hairs with its hands, it listens to its parent's voice and other sounds, it smells body scents and tastes a little milk from its mother's breast. It also has passive experiences: it moves naturally with its parents breathing, and it is stroked and cuddled

Observational findings suggest it is a pleasurable experience for the child. It relaxes and has a contented expression. Following a period of sometimes extremely alert behaviour, it usually falls into a deep sleep characterised by a quiet and regular breathing pattern.

For parents the kangaroo method brings them

close to their baby; they feel at one with their child. The initial phase is often deeply emotional – for many parents it is the first time they have true physical contact with their child. The parents' self-confidence grows with time, and any anxieties they have are eased as their faith in the health of their child increases. Parental feelings are reinforced. Parents can feel their child next to them and really get to know it. They can stay happily dozing like this for hours. An additional positive side-effect is that breast-feeding, which is far more problematic following premature birth, is greatly stimulated by the kangaroo method

The kangaroo method is widespread in the Netherlands. Nonetheless, too little attention is given to it on many incubator wards. All too often, objections are raised in order to discourage it, obstruct it or even forbid it. And only rarely is the kangaroo method truly encouraged, let alone taken for granted as a right.

A red baby sling for the best singer in the village

Chapter 1.5

The meaning of colours, motifs and materials

A. Tabak

'Unknown symbols are eight thousand years old' read the headline to a newspaper article in January 1991. It concerned a book by the British archaeologist James Mellaart, *The Goddess from Anatolia*. In it he argues that Turkish carpet weavers use motifs that date back to the Stone Age. Nobody knew where these motifs originated until Mellaart discovered a number of Neolithic frescoes. Modern stylised motifs appeared to have come from them.

Many symbols that we do not understand – or no longer understand – can be found on slings used for carrying babies. Their meanings are complex, they are concerned with both profane and religious aspects of existence, they are expressions of physical protection or benediction, and they indicate the social rank of a mother and child. Only after studying the population using a particular design, and the significance they attach to colour, form and material, can we 'read' the sling.

The meanings of colours in a sling correspond to the general meaning given to those colours within a particular culture. These meanings are bound up with material circumstances such as physical environment, time structure, natural forces, scarcity and abundance. The Inuit, who live in Greenland and Canada, have twenty names for variations in the colour we call white; many gradations of it are found in their natural environment. Among some native North American tribes too, the significance of particular colours is determined by their surroundings – the mountainous terrain in which they live changes hue throughout the day and night. Black represents darkness; blue, sunrise; white, daytime; and yellow, dusk. They also use these four colours to describe the four points of the compass: the Black Mountains to the west, the Blue Mountains to the south, the White Mountains to the east, and the Yellow Mountains to the west.

To the indigenous Craho population of Brazil, red signifies femininity, and black, masculinity. They use a red dye made from extracts of the Uruku plant and black charcoal to colour their slings. Only the village's best singer is permitted to use a red sling, and then only for her first child. The same tint of red is used for the death ritual, during which the medicine man first paints his own face red and then that of the deceased. Peruvian slings also frequently feature red and black in addition to other colours. Here the two colours refer to the huayruro bean. The ancient Inca used this bean as protection against malign spirits.

In Japan red kimonos may be used for carrying babies. They are used exclusively for baby girls. The red dye is obtained from the beni-bana plant (American saffron) and originally offered protection from insects. This colour also protects against evil. The colour red is associated with blood and femininity, and this has led to its use for girls. Especially in Western Europe, pink is the colour used for girls, and blue for boys.

The meanings of motifs are less consistent than those of colours. Dyes are obtained from the local environment and often remain in use for centuries and hence their meanings are often also preserved. Motifs, on the other hand, can be changed fairly easily, because of internal changes, or external forces. Although many motifs are ancient, their meanings change with time, and are closely bound up with the particular phase of development of a culture. For this reason, it is possible that the original meaning is lost. This is especially true of originally religious symbols that continue to be used only for profane or decorative purposes.

Motifs are incorporated into textile decorations. They may be woven, left undyed (using *batik*, *ikat* and *plangi* techniques), printed, embroidered, or sewn on, according to local methods of textile production. If a particular culture has a highly developed weaving tradition, then the motifs on slings will be woven. Motifs can therefore vary widely according to region.

Sling motifs are ultimately less consistent than colouring because fashion and the personal taste of the carrier or maker influences the design. It is therefore possible to recognise variations in motifs and designs according to the era, region and style in which they were made. However, this requires a thorough knowledge of local cultural history.

The meanings of motifs used on clothing and slings are largely determined by the social environment. The relationship between human and animal is of central importance in hunting, gathering and fishing peoples. Animal worship plays a great role in hunting cultures. Animal motifs form the ancient basis of their symbolic languages: depictions of the predators that threaten their existence, and the prey that provides sustenance. When an animal behaves like a human, it is considered a rival. When an animal has characteristics that humans wish to possess, there is a contradiction. Generally, hunting and fishing peoples use animal motifs on textiles and clothing, but gatherers do not. Gatherers normally use multifunctional slings or nets, and their clothing is usually minimal.

Chinese baby carrier (detail left) inscribed with the motto 'work hard and make progress every day'.
[Property of the author]

Food crops are as important to agrarian peoples as game animals are to hunters. They have many rituals associated with horticulture and agriculture. The motifs they use in their visual language can be traced to crops and medicinal plants. Farmers also use stylised human figures as motifs.

Herders and nomads use motifs from hunting and early arable farming cultures. The motifs associated with hunting relate to geographical and natural phenomena, and to the rhythms of the seasonal and daily cycles. Changes in the natural environment often have a direct impact on the daily lives of roaming peoples, if for no other reason than that they determine their herds', and thus their own, movements. Natural phenomena are more difficult to depict than animals or plants, and for this reason, motifs relating to them are often highly stylised. Such decorations are characteristic of herding and nomadic peoples. Furthermore, the form of the motifs is connected to the herding animals they eat. Arable farmers with cattle stock use identical motifs.

In modern industrial society there is no direct relationship between motif and meaning. Motifs may be derived from any other culture, depending on the aesthetic awareness, fashion and social group of the bearer. Not all motifs are incorporated into the fabric used for slings: we may find any motifs that perpetuate life, but none related to death.

Motifs that are frequently used can have the following functions: to wish for good fortune, to ensure the well-being and protection of a child, or to indicate gender, the social status of the person carrying the child and the territory in which manufacture took place.

Each culture uses certain motif groups, which I call *core motifs*. They may have the same form among different cultures but their meaning can change according to social economic factors, religion, habitat and decoration techniques. Sling motifs can be created from diverse materials applied as decoration to the cloth, and appear in a variety of colour combinations. They may be woven in, sewn on, embroidered, stamped, painted, carved or burnt in.

The motifs can be classified as follows: geometric motifs (lines, circles, triangles, squares, pentagrams and meanders), plant motifs (trees, flowers and crops), animal motifs (insects, birds, fish, reptiles, mammals and mythical creatures) and letter motifs (monograms and pictographs).

Geometric motifs

Lines used on slings in the Andes indicate lines in the landscape. Zigzag stripes mean that the bearer comes from the mountains, for example. And this is also the case among the Nuba in Africa, but if the zigzag shapes comprise filled triangles they symbolise women's breasts. In Egypt zigzag motifs represent water.

The meaning of the line has changed in Europe over the last few centuries. In mediaeval times the use of lines in designs was taboo because they denoted the devil. This gradually changed, especially following the use of lines in the symbol of the American struggle for independence, the Stars and Stripes, and the use of lines by French revolutionaries, or

1. Development of the sun-wheel motif

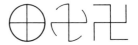

2. Meander motifs:

Peru – step border

Greek – Cretan

Sanculottes. The striped prison uniform is a reminder in modern times of the former negative association.

The frequently occurring meander, or continuous edge motif, represents the sun. It is based on the sun wheel, a circle containing a cross. In stages, this motif evolved first into an interrupted circle and then into what we recognise today as the swastika, originally a Buddhist symbol of good fortune. It is encountered particularly in Southeast Asia, and also in Lapland in northern Europe and among the Maya in America (fig. 1).

Meander motifs with the same meaning are also found in South America. Here they are stepped squares. In the Mediterranean region, meanders are derived from waves (fig. 2). And geometric motifs based on inextricable knots are found in Africa and Southeast Asia. These, just like the meander, represent the eternal continuance of existence. Many Islamic weavings feature triangles with a small vertical line, which can be traced, as a pictograph, to the Sumerian symbol for woman, from 2600 BC (fig. 3).

The five-pointed star motif, the pentagram, is found throughout the world. It is very ancient – older than writing – and it was used by the Babylonians. Pentagrams are also used as stylisations of stars and flowers, or rosettes (fig. 4).

Circles are found on Japanese carrying-kimonos. Here, they are stylised representations of balls of wool, representing children's toys (fig. 5).

Plant motifs

In northern Europe the tree of life is painted on carry-cots, in Japan the pine tree is used, and in Egypt, the olive tree. The tree is the sign for long life, and in Japan and Egypt this is amplified by its association with the colour green. In the Caucasus, the tree forms a connection between the underworld and the living world. Their representation of the world

3. Female motifs

Turkish; Siberian

Caucasian; Phoenician

Turkmeni, Neolithic goddess figures.

4. Pentagrams

5. Japanese circle motifs.

consists of three layers separated horizontally. The upper area represents the sun; the central area, containing a tree, symbolises the living world; and the lower layer, the underworld. Originally a shamanic view of the world, it has been preserved in Islamic motifs.

In Guatemala, patterns formed with stylised maize plant motifs, a food crop, are used on slings. It is a sign of the maize goddess and in this context it is a fertility symbol (fig. 6).

The pomegranate protruding from a vase represents female fertility, and this motif is widespread – from Persia to Central Europe. Pomegranates, flowers and twigs coming out of hearts can mean long life and abundance.

Flower motifs are frequently used for slings, added purely decoratively or as an expression of a wish for good fortune or well-being. In China, Japan and Indonesia, flower motifs were originally Buddhist symbols of happiness. The lotus blossom stands for summer, young married couples, and rebirth. Chrysanthemums and twigs indicate autumn, winter and old women. The peony rose represents spring and girls.

Japanese women carry the sling under a capacious kimono. A motif is embroidered on the back of the kimono that indicates the baby's gender: a flower for a girl and an arrow flight for a boy (fig. 7).

6. Maize meanders: Ixahuacan; Guatemala.

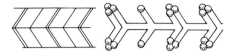

7. Japanese embroidered motifs: girl; boy

8. Kutchin bead motifs: dog paw; ptarmigan foot; beaver seed, running mouse.

Rosette designs are derived from pentagrams. The Kutchin, an Alaskan people, have a rosette with a special form. The straps they make to carry their children indicate the social ranking of the parents. The name of the child is embroidered in the middle of the strap with beads. They are additionally decorated with mainly rosette motifs, also using beads. These floral designs have animal names (fig. 8). A rosette with four leaves is called the dogs foot, a rosette with three leaves is the called a Ptarmigan (a bird belonging to the grouse family) foot, a rosette with one leaf is called beaver seed, and a chain of leaves is called a running mouse. It is notable that the names are older than the motifs.

Important among the core motifs are the animal motifs, which may include depictions of both real and imagined animals – the mythical Chinese phoenix, for example, which suggests femininity, and symbolises a long life and happy marriage. Also in China, the dragon is the male sign for rain and the fertility of the earth. Baby carriers used in Shidong feature dragons and phoenix good-luck charms surrounded by flowers, birds, insects and fish.

Real birds, such as ducks and geese, also symbolise happiness. Butterflies and cranes are good omens. In Anatolia and Finland, the peacock represents marriage and motherhood, and in Iran, the heron means long life. The mythical Indonesian Garuda, or sun bird, stands for happiness, and is sometimes depicted only as a stylised wing, or *lar*, motif, as in Java (fig. 9).

The Siberian Khanty paint a small bird on the head end of their carry-cots because they believe that a child will fall asleep when a bird alights on their cot. The bird also protects the child's dreams. Birds of prey have power ascribed to them; they possess coveted characteristics. The eagle and the condor represent conquest and courage, and the owl, wisdom. Two opposing ducks mean doubled happiness in China, while two condors means doubled power in South America. In Europe and Anatolia, two birds symbolise the combination of love and fidelity.

The Miao people in the West Hunan province of China inhabit an environment highly populated by snakes, and they were frequently bitten by them. The straps they used to carry babies feature snake motifs and designs, which offer protection against these attacks. On the eastern Indonesian island of Sumba, snakes are a traditional motif; they symbolise the life-and-death cycle because they shed their skin, as do shrimps. And elsewhere in

9. Larmotief (vleugels van Garudavogel).

10. Slangmotieven: Bolivia; gevederde slangen Andes.

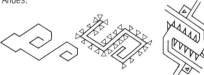

11. Reindeer motifs: Lapland; North Siberia; Ostyak; North Siberia.

12. Motif woven in as an amulet. Carrier bag, East Anatolia.
[Photograph Josephine Powell]

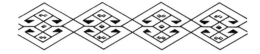

Indonesia the scales of the snake Naga protect against evil and disease. The stylised woven snake motifs of Bolivia often depict a feathered serpent. Alternatively, flowers grow out of the snake, and it is transformed into a cornfield. The feathered serpent is an ancient Mayan divinity (Quetzalcoatl) encountered as a motif throughout the Andes. The divine-serpent motif is found from Taiwan to Peru and is associated with the blessings and powers of life and growth that it brings (fig. 10).

The highly stylised depictions of reindeer antlers from Lapland and Siberia are symbols of power. They are carved into beech wood carry-cots and embroidered on blankets for the baby (fig. 11).

Incantations and benedictions also appear, in the form of pictographs or letters of the alphabet. A machine-manufactured sling from China features characters forming the motto 'work hard, and make progress every day'

Decorations and motifs that are applied as a constituent of the material appear in most cases to be symbols of good fortune and indicators of social rank. Sometimes, the motif has a protective function, and thus serves as an amulet (Anatolia, fig. 12), which summons a force field that is capable of resisting unseen powers. This function bridges the distinction between this and the final classification: the material.

For practical reasons, carry-cots are usually made of locally obtainable light materials, such as textile, bark, wood, twine or leather. Materials used for decoration – shells, beads, (precious) metals and precious stones – are often imported or have great or particular value in the region, and also often function as amulets. If made from human or animal material they can imbue the bearer with the characteristics of that animal or person, and protect from evil. They sometimes have a medical, or therapeutic, function. Using these, a nursing infant may teethe without pain. In former times, parents in Europe used the cuckoo flower and red-coral necklaces for the same purpose. In South Africa necklaces made from a seed named 'tooth pearl' are used. Such amulets need not be worn visibly. The Inuit, for example, attach the child's umbilical cord to its *amauti*, providing it with power, health and a long life. Alternatively, a small piece of

Inuit on the east coast of Greenland (see also page 132). White is an important colour to them.
[Photograph B. Robbe, 1972]

used brown slings and others had white ones. She set about researching the matter thoroughly. Did the colours indicate differences in status or gender perhaps? Did they have a religious significance? The clue for the reception was in the material that was used – wool. After much thought the carriers themselves provided the solution. Women with brown slings had brown sheep, and women with white slings had white ones.

This leather baby carrier from Senegal is decorated with bottles of butter, which is used to keep the baby's bottom soft.
[Photograph Musée de l'Homme, Paris]

flint may be sewn into a pouch in order that the stone's power resist fire. A modern-day version of this custom is the placing of a box of matches in the cradle by Siberian parents.

In the Islamic world, blue beads protect women and children against the evil eye, and red coral is an ancient defence against evil spirits. The word 'bead' is derived from the Old English word for prayer, *beðan*, because of the use of rosary beads in prayer in the Catholic religion. The Egyptian word for bead is *shasha*, meaning 'happiness and prosperity', and the Arabic word for bead necklace is *tsbiah*, which means 'commemorate God by prayer'.

In the Caucasus, Iran and Lapland, silver and gold bells are hung on carry-cots. The objects have a threefold material significance: they are useful because the sound they produce relaxes the child, they protect the child by frightening away demons, and they denote status because they are signs of affluence.

Baby carriers are symbol carriers. However, just how difficult it can be for an outsider to gain insight into sling motifs is illustrated by the following story. In a remote village in the Andes, a researcher noted that some women

Part 2

Cradleboard. Tandjong Karang, Central Borneo, Indonesia, decorated with wood carvings. Attached to the cradleboard are shells, beads, dog teeth and food bundles to protect the child from evil influences and to attract benign spirits.

[Museum of Ethnology Collection, Leiden]

Mother with sleeping child. Nigeria.
[Photo G. Kocher, Musée de l'Homme, Paris]

Chapter 2.1.1

Equatorial Africa

Dazzling colours on an antelope skin

M. de Lataillade

The child is being carried in a bag of untanned antelope leather. Cameroon.
[Photograph H. Nègre, Musée de l'Homme, Paris]

The image of a mother carrying a baby on her back or hip is a classic representation of African womanhood. The child is carried in a hip-cloth or carrier designed for the purpose. Throughout the continent, in rural and urban areas alike, mothers carry their children with an ease that astounds Western women. African women carry their children not only for practical earthly reasons, but also to protect them from supernatural dangers.

In general, to become a mother is the highest priority for an African woman. It is a form of value appreciation; her descendants will continue her own or her husband's line – depending on the family system operating – and they ensure survival. A woman that brings a child into the world provides the family with important advantages, both social and economic.

Thus, pregnancy is greeted with joy and relief in almost all African communities. All efforts are made to protect the expected baby. The mother takes the precaution of hiding the fact that she is pregnant for as long as possible; supernatural forces that have been so well-disposed to her must not be displeased. Still today, even in large cities, a woman will prefer not to discuss her pregnancy. She makes cautious preparations for the arrival of her child. She must observe many taboos. These vary according to community, and often relate to food and to sex. To contravene any of these rules may be disastrous, and so bring both her own life and her child's in danger.

Rituals practiced at birth and in the ensuing period relate to special care for the newborn, the destination of the placenta, the period of postnatal seclusion (which may vary between a few weeks and a few months, depending on the community), the taboos surrounding the new mother, and the naming of the newborn, whereby it is accepted into the group.

Following delivery, the mother resumes her normal life once more. In the meantime, she has attained the status of mother within the community, and enjoys the attendant prestige. She will keep her child with her night and day for the foreseeable future. As long as the child is nursing, it remains part of the 'other world', and it is fervently hoped that it will not wish to return there. Namegiving alone does not entitle a child to full acceptance into the human world. By keeping it with her at all times – during the night against her on the sleeping mat, and during daytime on her back –

she minimises any risks and keeps evil spirits at bay. In the meantime, she provides the child with all its daily requirements.

An infant that needs be in close proximity to its mother must be carried by the most comfortable possible method. Initially, it is wrapped in a carrying cloth, but as soon as the baby can hold its own head up, it is carried on the back or on the hip. A great variety of baby carriers exist. Examples in the Musée de l'Homme in Paris show that there are marked differences between them, and that these differences are determined largely by the region and the period in which they were made. Following namegiving, the Dogon of Mali made large slings from strips of fabric. Anthropologist Germaine Dieterlen noted that these strips displayed some unusual features: 'the newborn child comes out of the amniotic fluid, which one is reminded of by the slings' blue background colour. The slings consist of a row of strips, one for the first child, two for the second child, and so forth. Some strips they use in slings for children born in special circumstances, such as children born to women who had not menstruated since giving birth to their previous child, or twins and triplets. Nobility of the Kuno people use strips of material with one red stripe if a single child is born, and with two stripes when twins are born. The red pigment used for the stripes contains some of the child's blood. The blood symbolises the sacrifices that have been made at the altar of Kuno (*Symbolism in Textiles, West Africa* exhibition, Germaine Dieterlen collection, Musée de l'Homme, 1977).

Many baby carriers are made of specially prepared animal skins. Either a type of rucksack or straps for carrying the child on the hip are made from this supple material. The straps are intended for women who need only walk short distances or for those who already have a basket on their back.

Some baby carriers in Africa are woven from plant fibres. One of these was initially

known by the name 'Important Pilgrim'. The anthropologist Eric de Dampierre recognised it as a baby carrier originating in Oubangi, and brought it from the Congo in 1873. It is constructed from rectangular pieces of finely woven and openwork raffia approximately 70cm by 90cm. In the middle there is a slit with scalloped raffia edging. At each end there is a handful of hard bound plant fibres.

A baby carrier made by the Kawaka group in Sudan is made from a piece of extremely tough buffalo hide. The carrier is covered with red pigment and has four securing straps. It is almost square (27cm wide, 26 to 28cm long, 33cm at the centre), slightly concave, with the edges beaten out and glued together. The four carrying-straps are attached at the corners. The leather is entirely covered with dots in relief.

Traditional decorations were used by the maker of this child carrier. The seeds of wild and cultivated plants have replaced beads, which are sold to tourists and are thus hard to come by. The decorations are combined with aluminium chains – separate or in parallel rows – a piece of zip fastener and multicoloured beads. Much attention is paid to the symmetry of the colours.
[M. Delaplanche, Musée de l'Homme, Paris]

J.P. Lebeuf found another, equally impressive, baby carrier during an expedition in Cameroon. It is made and used by the Fali, who live in the north of the country. It is a rectangle of supple leather, approximately 26cm by 42cm. Along the upper edge is a 5cm-wide decorative band consisting of two rows of dried round seeds, and the carrying straps are attached at each corner. This 'bag' is decorated with a double row of dried black pods from a bean plant. On the right-hand side are ten fine strips of leather onto which seeds have been sewn.

Another frequently encountered design comprises a number of straps made of antelope hide. The woman wears it as a sling over her shoulder, with the child on her hip. The Musée de l'Homme in Paris has a good example in its collection that was brought by the missionary, Broc, from the Fang, who inhabit Gabon. There are two hard and hairless leather straps about 77cm in length and 8cm in width. These are attached to each other by means of thin strips of leather. A third strap, only 60cm long, connects the other two, creating a seat for the child.

The child carriers made by the Bassari in Senegal are also renowned. They are made either from antelope skin made pliant with palm oil, or goatskin. The hair is on the outside of the carrier. The design is unchanging: a pentagon whose top corner is beaten down over the furred side creating a smooth triangle contrasting with the furred background. In this way a trapezium is created. A long leather loop is attached to the ends of the short lower horizontal side of this trapezium, which the mother puts over her head. Two other straps are attached to the longer horizontal side; these hold the loop in place on the chest and are fastened around the waist. The carrier is decorated with a number of carefully selected ornaments: brightly coloured strings of beads, small pieces of silver-coloured metal, buttons, fabrics, seeds, pieces of plastic and so on. This exuberant and harmonious combination of colours makes the baby carriers both dazzling and elegant.

The father of the child makes the baby carrier. Should a woman divorce and remarry while pregnant from the first partner, the new husband communicates this to the first, who subsequently makes the child carrier and brings it to the woman and her new husband.

Two or three baby carriers are used by each child as it grows during the first couple of years of life. They do not wear out quickly, however, and are passed from child to child. Antelope hide is used for the youngest babies and goatskin for the others.

When a mother sits, she usually lays her child on the ground. She often wears the empty carrier as a headband, with the inner leather or cotton strap over her forehead. The extremely sturdy securing straps may be made from dried and stripped chimpanzee skin.

Children play with toy versions of baby carriers. They strongly resemble the genuine article, but are slightly less beautifully finished and are always made of goatskin. Decorations are equally carefully selected and just as exuberant. They are made using shells, glass and wooden beads, aluminium and pieces of zips.

Children are usually carried on their mother's back, but there are other ways to transport the child, as shown by the baskets on the heads of women in Burkina Faso. Whichever method they choose, their freedom of movement remains great. They are not restricted by the presence of their newborn baby. They can go where they want and go about their daily duties. They can even take part in dances, while taking great care of their child's welfare.

Chapter 2.1.2

Ghana and Nigeria

A long tradition

B. Menzel

In 1961 I visited West Africa for the first time, as part of investigation into traditional crafts. Among all the other new sights that impressed themselves upon me, I noticed that many people – men and women, boys and girls – carried loads on their heads. Only the women had an additional burden: a child. The combined weight of the baby and the generally heavy packages they carried on their heads was no doubt considerable.

I would have liked to have made further studies of this interesting method of transporting children. Alas, the time available to me for research was much too limited. However, during this and later visits until 1992, I took as many photographs and notes as I could.

Slowly but surely, my records grew. Certain patterns became evident, but also notable disparities. I wish to present some of my material here, as my modest contribution to this crucial aspect of life in Africa.

The information shared with me by so many women related not only to their own personal experiences, but was also derived from oral tradition. When artists create representations of human figures, they often taken great care to reflect characteristic details accurately. Asante goldweights in particular offer us a wealth of details, which in general correspond with those obtained from the oral tradition. Such sources provide an extremely clear and consistent illustration of many aspects of baby and toddler care.[1]

Common to all cultures I have obtained information about is the special treatment of young mothers and their newborn babies for the first seven days after delivery. This is doubtless based on centuries-old experience. Although they differ in many ways from one another the Asante, Ebira, Fante, Hausa and many others, strictly adhere to a period of rest in isolation. The namegiving ceremony takes place only after this critical period, and a child is only carried on someone's back for the first time on the eighth day.

Carrying is performed with extreme care. The umbilical cord will usually have fallen off during the seven days of isolation, but the navel will still be sensitive. The back of the person who will carry the child for the first time – usually one of the grandmothers – is covered with extremely soft material such as old rags. These are generally given by the father or grandmother, as are the nappy cloths. In earlier times, the Asante used *baha* fibres obtained from the trunk of the plantain tree for this purpose.

---

[1] With thanks to my many and patient instructors whom I met on visits to Ghana and Nigeria between 1961 and 1992, and also to my old friends Amy Badoe Agyeman in Accra and Florence Dede Hin-Ankrah in Leiden.

Once the woman's back is covered with this soft material, she leans forward in order that the naked baby can be laid down, its chest on her back. The cloth is placed over the baby's back, under the woman's arms and tied at the front. In this way, the baby is securely and entirely wrapped in the cloth, apart from its head. Attention is paid to the position of the baby's head: it must be turned sideways in order for it to breathe freely. The cloth is fastened in such a way that all the weight pulls on the place where the cloth is fastened, just above the breasts. The bottom of the cloth is also fastened at the front of the body. No buttons are used.

Traditional women's clothing consists of shawls that are fastened by overlapping the two ends. The outer end is stuffed between the inner end and the body. Women are so adept at this technique that their clothing never loosens unexpectedly. This is not the case among young, less experienced, girls. For safety's sake, if they have to carry a child an extra length of fabric is pulled around the baby and girl's midriff, where it is knotted.

Contact between mother and child was most complete when women still dressed in the traditional manner, in a cache-sexe or a short cloth wrapped around the waist. A longer variant of this wrap is tied at the armpits and extends to the ankles, which considerably reduces skin contact between mother and baby. The adoption of the blouse or shirt as an item of clothing for women prevents skin contact between mother and child, although of course bodily contact remains close. This close contact has a strong effect if the child is unwell or discontented. When taken onto the back, it generally becomes quiet and quickly falls asleep. The soothing effect may be intensified by the mother tapping gently on the baby's bottom.

The young mother taking care of her first child has already built up experience with younger brothers and sisters. She will nonetheless need the help of another woman to tie a newborn child onto her own back for as long as the child is weak and difficult to manoeuvre. An experienced mother has no need for assistance. It is astonishing how quickly she can transfer a baby in her arms to her back. To avoid any chance of the child sliding from her back, she leans forward a little and pushes the child under her arm. The most comfortable position must then be achieved with some readjustments. The baby's head should be between the mother's

Female Asante mourners during the ceremonies in remembrance of the death of the Omanhene Kamuwu (the King of Kamuwu). Red symbolises sorrow. Kamawu, Ghana, 1974.

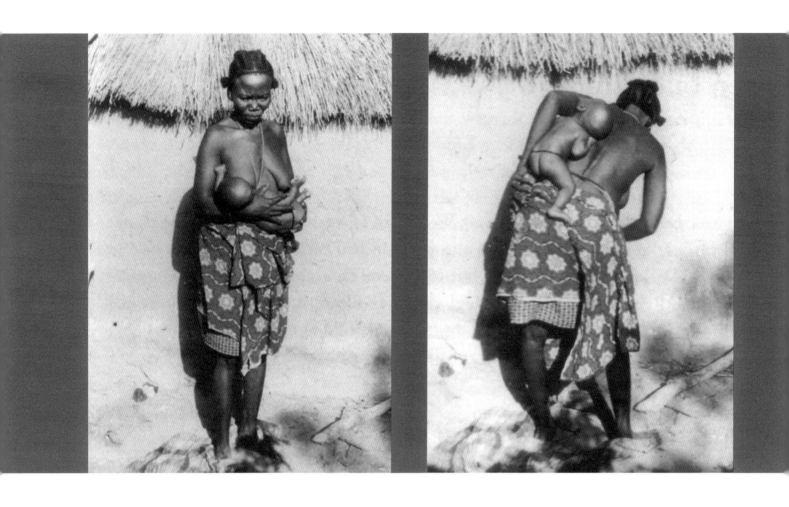

shoulder blades and its bodyweight at the spine. Balance is important: the baby's limbs stretch out to each side - first the legs, then the arms. The mother then takes hold of the cloth, folds it around the child and her own back, pulls it around the front and secures the top and bottom by tucking in the corners. The operation takes less than five minutes.

As long as the mother remains at home she will generally carry her child in a single sling. She may choose to also use an additional shawl, knotted at the front, for extra support. Outside, a second cloth is worn around both her and the baby. It is secured only at the top of the front, and hangs loosely, like a dress.
    Small babies are entirely covered by the cloth, as are those who are unwell. Unless it is cold or the mother has to make a long journey, from the age of around four months the baby's arms and legs are kept out of the cloth.

This method of carrying babies is extremely practical. Although generally positioned at the centre of the mothers back, the child can easily be manoeuvred to one side or even to the front while remaining safely in the cloth. There are, however, a number of preventative measures that the mother must take in order to protect the child on her back. She must take care that its nose is not pressed against her back, and when in a crowded area she shifts the child to one side and protect its head under her arm. She must also ensure that she does not cause the child to become too warm by wrapping it in too dark a fabric, or wearing a headscarf that drapes over the child's face, for example. Such a headscarf will also flap around in the slightest breeze, and care must be taken to protect the baby's face from this.

The Asante have a strong tradition of colour symbolism. The use of colour to express posi-

tive or negative feelings is still widespread today. Red and white are opposing colours: red represents sorrow, and white, all that is positive: joy, victory and purity. The arrival of a baby creates an opportunity to wear white, to rejoice in the victory of mother and child over all the dangers of pregnancy and delivery. The white material for the sling and white clothing for the mother may be gifts from the father or family, or she may buy them herself. During the namegiving ceremony, mother and child are painted with splendid patterns using white clay. Women also wear white during services of thanks in church for a successful birth.

In earlier times, the white cloth was used to carry the baby for its first three months, but gradually it is becoming customary to use it for six months. For reasons of hygiene, midwives and clinics naturally, and gratefully, take advantage of the symbolic value of white to encourage the use of white fabrics in childcare.

At a later stage in the baby's development, any fabric may be called into service as a sling. Only among the Asante is the use of white material during the baby's first months compulsory. The type and size of cloth that is used for carrying babies cannot be distinguished from that used for women's wraps.

Only the women of western Nigeria use a cloth for carrying a child that is made specifically for that purpose. This length of fabric is woven on an upright loom, as illustrated on page 44. Since time immemorial, the various population groups have each had their own style and their own terms for their textile baby carriers. The most productive weavers, Yoruba women, have created a market for their type of baby sling. Their word for it, *oja*, is not only a trade name, but has become the generic term for baby slings in the region. It has displaced the terms used for similar objects in other lan-

Returning from the market, this Esan woman carries three loads. Ewto, western Nigeria, 1992.

is applied as a compact strip over the middle of the cloth. The loops are sometimes cut open, creating a nap – apparently a relatively new development. The cloth is worn in such a way that the loop or plush side is visible.[2]

If a woman in western Nigeria wears a white cloth with loops, it means she has a child. Even if she wears it as a sash around her middle, the *oja* is no ordinary article of clothing. Should one see a woman wearing such a cloth but carrying no child, one can be sure that it is somewhere nearby.

Partly due to the stiffness of the rather thick, hand-woven cloth, no more than a half-knot is necessary to secure it in the front of the body. There is an interesting difference between the ways in which Asante and Fante women on the one hand, and western Nigerian Yoruba, Ebira and Esan women on the other, carry their children. The former wear the sling under their wrap, while the latter wear it as their outermost item of clothing.

Ojas are sold by individual weavers, on the market, at the roadside or by travelling merchants. In the spring of 1992, I bought a white *oja* woven from cotton and synthetic yarn and decorated with tufts, from a woman with a stall on the Auchi-Jattu Road, for 35 Naira, the equivalent of about 3 euros. She told me that all baby slings at her stall had been woven by Egara, or Igarra, women. In 1976, I bought a splendidly woven carrying cloth, featuring a woven-in loop design, at the Maiduguri market for 1 Naira and 5 shillings. The stallholder called it an *abin goyo*, which means 'a thing for carrying children on the back' in Hausa. This cloth originated in Yoruba country. It would be interesting to study how far the Yoruba word *oja* has spread, and when it took place.

The preparation of a child for the tasks it will later perform begins early. Even in play, the traditional division of labour between women and men is evident. Although boys as well as girls will take care of their smaller brothers

guages, such as the word *ugbakun* in the language of the Esan.

Traditionally, the *oja* is woven from hand-spun cotton thread. Cotton was cultivated locally in varieties with white and brown fibres. Cotton twine dyed with indigo was sometimes used to create woven decorations. Nowadays, industrially produced yarn is used almost exclusively. There is clearly an increasing tendency to use synthetic yarn in combination with cotton. Synthetic fibres are, after all, cheaper, stronger and easier to wash. One disadvantage to the use of synthetic materials is that the slings can be too warm for the baby.

In addition to the use of coloured thread for decoration, looped pile fabric is also popular. It

---

[2] See also *Techniques in Nigeria*, p 140.

and sisters and men may carry a child on the arm, shoulder or hip, childcare is generally the responsibility of women and girls. Only they carry babies on their backs.

It is sometimes impossible to distinguish between games that girls play with dolls and their first exercises in childcare. A four-year-old girl may well be asked to assist in looking after the baby, under the supervision of the mother. In time, both children will be permitted to walk around together, the baby on the child's back. Although the girl will have some experience carrying her dolls, an adult will assist in securing the baby to her back.

While the baby is nursing, the older sister may not wander far from home. She must be able to return quickly should the baby become restless. Later, when it is not entirely dependent on breast milk she may attempt to settle it herself with a tasty titbit before returning.

The baby will rapidly become too heavy to be carried on the back by a child only a few years older than itself. As soon as the baby can sit upright and keep its head up, it is carried on the hip.

Twins are welcome, but provide logistical challenges for their mother: safe transportation, for example. The customary method of conveying children requires that the weight be centred on the spine. For this reason, twins are never carried together on one woman's back. If both children need their mother's attention, one is carried on the back and the other is taken on the arm (usually the left) against the shoulder, or alternatively on the hip. Sometimes a woman carries two children in the baby sling, but only for short periods or distances; for long distances a second person will be asked to assist, often an older sister.

Newborn babies are only carried on the back for short periods. The lengths of these periods increase gradually as the child develops, and eventually it may be carried for several hours at a time if necessary. The child develops a

Instead of a baby, a Hausa girl fastens a wooden stool to her back. Anka, North Nigeria 1961.

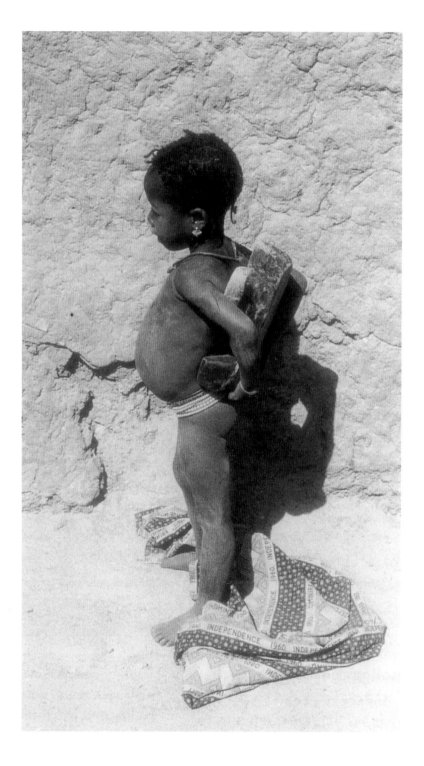

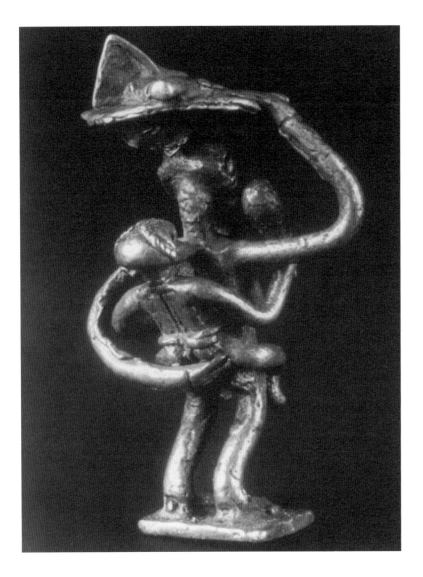

without any support on the mother's back. That the absence of a baby sling is no omission on the part of the goldsmith, is indicated by the child apparently being strong enough to hold onto its mother's back, support itself and even carry a calabash of water or porridge.

Only when the baby is big enough to take food other than milk, can the young mother enjoy a little more freedom of movement: she is then no longer the only source of sustenance for the child. Two years is considered the appropriate age for weaning. Traditionally, a woman only then resumes her marital duties. The lengthy period of sexual abstinence is seen as necessary in order to prevent the well-being of the newborn from being threatened by a new pregnancy. For the time that she is the sole, or primary, source of nutrition for her child, the mother has to take her child with her everywhere she goes: to her work, on visits to friends and to ceremonies; whether formal or festive.

Small children are so used to being carried on the back that they are unperturbed by sudden movements or jolts. They either look around contentedly, or they sleep, equally contentedly. Many women's activities last the entire day. Often, in addition to the child on her back, she will have a load on her head; the total weight may be more than 30 kilos.[3]

If a woman is walking with a heavy load on her head and the baby on her back is crying, but there is no one with her who can help remove it or replace the load, she must walk on. She might attempt to calm it by talking softly or patting it gently on the bottom. However, if the child is hungry, the mother will attempt to shuffle it forward while walking so that it can drink. This manoeuvre is more difficult for older babies whose limbs are outside the sling, but the mother will attempt to get it into a position where it can get hold of a breast and drink from it.

strong sense of balance and the ability to clamp its legs to its mother's back like tongs. This surprisingly forceful clamping movement can be felt as an immediate reflex on picking up a child to sit it on one's hip. A toddler can even be carried on the back without the sling: the mother will sometimes support it with one or perhaps both arms.

This method of carrying, so much part of modern everyday life, is also often depicted by goldweights in the form of a woman and child making their way to the fields. This demonstrates the care and attention to detail with which Asante goldsmiths approached their illustrations of people. Although the baby is sometimes portrayed in a sling, usually it is

The mother develops a high sensitivity to the mood and welfare of the child on her back. She immediately recognises, for example, any advance signal of an impending bowel movement. Although toilet training begins very early and mishaps seldom occur, there are situations, as described above, in which the mother is unable to take any action. She must accept the consequences and there is nothing she can do about it until she reaches her destination.

A newborn baby sits relatively high on its mother's back, and as it grows it will eventually sit at the centre of the back. When she sits with her baby so low on her back it appears as if the baby is resting on a special seat. This is probably the source of a misunderstanding: that women added padding to their buttocks to provide a seat for the child. It was known as the 'bustle' in nineteenth century European fashion and is known as *atofo* in Asante. In fact, the *atofo* has nothing to do with the carrying of children, but is part of the traditional attire of women.

The carrying of babies and toddlers on the back is an ancient tradition. Rapid and fundamental changes have taken place over the last decennia, and these have created wide divergences between rural and urban life. It is difficult, or even impossible, to maintain the traditional close bond between mother and child in the modern urban setting. But the carrying of children on the back will remain necessary, and will not disappear quickly.

---

[3] A newborn baby weighs approximately 3 kilos, and by six months of age this has roughly doubled. By the age of two, it will not weigh less than 12 kilos.

Chapter 2.1.3

Southern Africa

The father makes the carrier, but only after the birth

M. Brodie

A variety of peoples inhabit the southern part of Africa. The most ancient of these were the Khoi and the San. They intermingled with many Bantu groups that arrived in the region as part of the multiple waves of migration over a thousand-year period. The first Europeans established themselves at the southernmost tip of the continent 350 years ago. The Khoi and the San have left behind many traces of their existence in cave paintings found throughout the region, in local knowledge of plants and medicinal herbs, and in a wealth of traditions. Descriptions of the habits and rituals of the earlier inhabitants lead to the conclusion that the manner in which young children are carried has changed little over the centuries.

In ancient times, all clothing, whether for men or women, was made of animal skin. The child carrier was made from an especially soft dried skin. In order to carry a child, the skin was knotted around the mother's midriff, the baby was placed against her back and the skin pulled over the child. The mother then pulled the top of the skin under her arms to the front where the ends when knotted above her breasts. Blankets or other fabrics later replaced skins, but the carrying method remained the same. An exception to this rule is the method used by the Herero in Namibia. Herero mothers tied the two straps at the bottom of the dried skin (the back legs of the goat) around their hips. The mother took the child by an arm, lifted it onto her back and pushed it into the fleece bag. The skin was pulled over the baby's head, and the upper straps (the front legs of the goat – extended if necessary) were pulled over its shoulders and tied at the throat. To prevent any obstruction to breathing, the upper knot was pulled down and tied to the straps around her middle.

However a child is carried, it is most important that it suffers no discomfort and protected from any possible danger. Furthermore, it is essential that the child be kept in close proximity to the mother or another family member, should the child require food, safety or solace. The baby carrier should also ease travel and movement in general. Although the customary way of carrying babies in Southern Africa is remarkably simple, it meets all the above conditions. Its usefulness is equal to that of more complex carriers such as the papoose.

The conditions that have inspired cultures elsewhere to make more sophisticated carriers appear not to exist in this part of the world. The climate is mild – deep winter here is warmer than summertime in many other places – so there is no need for sturdy and warm baby carriers that protect against harsh weather. And some carriers are designed for walking long distances. They must be sturdy and secure, especially if they are to be carried by pack animals, but the largely sedentary peoples of

Southern Africa have no need for these. The longest journey a mother made in the normal course of events was a trip to a neighbouring village. She simply carried the baby on her back, in a supple and practical animal skin. And although nomadic, the Khoi and the San travelled only short distances each day.

The type of child carrier produced and used by any particular population group is, of course, determined to a large extent by the materials and skills at their disposal. The art of weaving was not known to the people of Southern Africa, and so clothing and baby carriers alike were made from animal skins. They were sewn together with thread made from tendons obtained from the necks of bovine animals or larger breeds of antelope. The fleeces were usually decorated with shells, pieces of carvings, animal teeth and, later, with glass beads introduced by foreign merchants. Baby carriers were also sometimes decorated, but to a limited degree. Too many sewn-on decorations might have impeded mother or child.

European merchants introduced woven fabrics. Most peoples in the region took to using imported blankets and other materials for their clothing. Those that came into closest contact with the Europeans, such as the Xhosa on the Eastern Cape, developed singular clothing styles based on textiles. Clothing for women consisted of a wraparound skirt, a short cape and an apron made from cotton or other light fabric. During colder weather, women wore blankets or large cloth wraps made of wool or thick cotton pulled over their shoulders and almost entirely covering the body. The baby was carried in a blanket rather than an animal skin. Despite the inroads made by Western fabrics, Ndebele women living in central Transvaal continue to wear leather aprons at the front and rear. A woven blanket, however, displaced the traditional goatskin cape. Most Sotho peoples in the region wear similar traditional clothing.

In remote areas, where European goods did not penetrate, animal hides remained the primary material for clothing. In these areas, women still use leather baby carriers. These include the Himba, who inhabit the far northwest of Namibia, and the remaining San groups, who still live out their lives as hunters in the vast deserts of Botswana and Namibia.

Although the use of leather for baby carriers has all but vanished, the symbolic significance of animal skins remains of great importance. For most Bantu peoples in Southern Africa in any case, the most important requirement is that it comes from an animal killed according to a particular ritual. This ritual is associated with pregnancy. When a woman falls pregnant, a goat, or a duiker antelope if available, is slaughtered. An *isidiya*, or pregnancy apron, is made from its skin.

The pregnant woman wears this apron knotted over her breasts and midriff. It supports her body somewhat and lends her dignity in the final months of pregnancy. Moreover, it is believed that the antelope's characteristics – speed and surefootedness – are transferred to the unborn child. The apron is decorated with copper buttons or pop fasteners – though preferably with the old copper beads once worn by distinguished women from prominent families. These large handmade beads were among the first decorative objects to be brought into the region by foreign merchants. Because they were bequeathed and inherited by generation after generation, they are viewed as ancestral jewels. The wealthiest families possess a set of twelve jewels, and these are sewn at the bottom of the isidiya. When the apron has fulfilled its function, the ornamentation is removed and the hide becomes the carrier for the newborn child.

Most other Bantu peoples make the baby carrier from the skin of an animal that is slaughtered after the mother and child's compulsory period of isolation. According to tradition, young mothers belonging to the Pondo

in the Eastern Cape province must stay in their huts for ten days following the birth of their child. Should the woman have to go outside for any reason, she is covered in blankets so that no man can see her. Males, including the woman's husband, may not enter her hut during this period. They would not wish to, because it is believed that seeing the new mother would cause a loss of power. Two days after the end of the period of isolation, the father slaughters a goat, and the *imbeleko*, or baby carrier, or is made from its skin. The word imbeleko is derived from *ukubeleka*, meaning 'to carry a child on the back'.

West Transvaal Tswana have a similar tradition, only the design is different. The pregnant woman continues her daily household duties for as long as possible. When it is time for the child to be born, she takes up residence in a purpose-built hut. Usually, the woman is alone when giving birth, but her mother, or sometimes another older female family member, waits outside and provides assistance if required. She repeatedly enters the hut to check that all is well. Following birth and the arrival of the placenta, the mother calls the midwife, who ties of the umbilical cord and cuts it. The placenta and any other traces of the birth are buried in the ground in front of the hut.

At the first new moon after the birth, the midwife takes the child outside and raises it up to the moon saying 'there is your moon'. At about this time, the husband or another male family member will slaughter a sheep, goat or calf. The bag used for carrying the newborn baby is made from the skin of this animal. The making of the baby carrier before birth is taboo – to do so would invite misfortune. 'You don't make a carrier for an unborn child' is a popular local saying.

The child sees the world over his mother's shoulder. The sling is secured tightly around the chest. Pondo, South Africa.
[Photograph E. Pasqier, Musée de l'Homme, Paris]

Urban drift has caused many traditional practices to fall into obscurity, but some customs are still observed. Especially those practices, precepts and prohibitions associated with birth and the ensuing period are still strictly observed.

Although the manner and means of carrying a child may be simple, both are rich in symbolism and significance. The birth of the baby and the skin in which it is carried are intimately associated with each other. The animal-skin baby carrier is an expression of the entire culture. Even when a blanket is used, taboos and standards are in force and all traditional ceremonies are performed. In urban areas too, animals are ritually killed as an offering of thanks.

Young girls are the most important helpers for young mothers. If the mother already has daughters herself, then they will help her. They baby-sit and carry the child just like their mother – on their back in a cloth tied at the front.

Although the custom is rarely practiced now, Ndebele women, living in central Transvaal, used to make special dolls with strings of glass beads. A woman who already had children herself would give one to a bride. This gift was intended to inspire the ancestors to encourage pregnancy.

Not far from the Ndebele lives a small Sotho population, the Ntwane. As part of the initiation ceremony that marks girls' transition to womanhood, their bodies are adorned with grass streamers. The older women who lead the ceremony tell them about the group's customs and traditions regarding menstruation, pregnancy and sexuality. At the end of the initiation period, which can last three months, a large thin doll resembling a phallus is made from a bundle of grass, and this is decked with grass garlands. Some of the bracelets worn by the girls are used in its making. Using the dolls, girls learn how they must carry their own children.

The Lesotho Sotho live in the southernmost Bantu region. During their wedding ceremony, brides wear a cone-shaped doll, its back decorated with beads. The doll receives a name that will later be given to the bride's first child.

These are no toy dolls then, for they have functions within the initiation rites, and clearly refer to the fertility of women. Their toy counterparts are usually made of a corn-cob by girls' mothers, and 'dressed' in fabric and beads. Girls play with these in much the same way as children elsewhere in the world, except that here they also carry the dolls on their backs. From the age of five or six they are allowed to carry real babies.

Europe

Chapter 2.2

For beggars, musicians, gypsies and hippies

E.M. Kloek

The carrying of babies in a sling or bag is viewed as an exotic habit in Western countries. The population at large have yet to be convinced that it is beneficial for a baby to be kept close to its parent's body, and references to ancient non-Western cultures may be necessary if this is to happen. Nonetheless, the baby carrier is slowly but surely gaining increasing acceptance as an element in parents' paraphernalia. In this chapter, I would like to pay closer attention to this generally unnoticed phenomenon.[1] Are slings, bags or baskets used to transport small children really so new to Western countries? If so, how were children carried in the past? When were baby carri-

ers introduced to Western culture and for what reasons?
In our quest, we discovered that baby carriers have never been the subject of historical research, which serves to illustrate how unfamiliar we are with the habit of carrying our children.

If one searches Western iconography for images of babies being carried, one soon encounters the Christian Madonna tradition. The number of portrayals of Mary and baby Jesus are countless. There are scarcely any of Mary with Jesus in a baby carrier of any kind, however. She is generally seen seated holding Jesus, and a mother would generally not require a sling in such a position. On the contrary, it is striking that Mary frequently appears to be holding Jesus somewhat awkwardly. Although, as artists emphasise, she is depicted as a loving mother, the image of the holy mother with her son, the Son of God, is primarily intended to instil awe and respect. A baby sling as an attribute would doubtless be considered too earthly. There is, however, one popular theme in the iconographic tradition surrounding Mary in which she is not static. This is because she is travelling – on the flight to Egypt. Mary and Joseph had to flee from King Herod, who had heard rumours of the birth of a new king (Jesus) and subsequently issued orders to kill all newborn sons. Artists have depicted the flight to Egypt many times. Here too, whether seated on a donkey or on grass, Mary carries her son in her arms. In early depictions of his journey, Joseph is also seen carrying Jesus – holding the child's feet as he sits on his shoulders (Vogler, 1930,

---

[1] With thanks to Anneke van Omme and Julie Houben. Thanks also to Vincent Boele, The Amsterdam Bible Museum, Bianca du Mortier, Rijksmuseum Amsterdam, E. Calje, KOG Amsterdam, Annemarie de Wildt, Amsterdam Historical Museum. The points of reference used in this section are limited to the Netherlands. Generally, two types of source material were used: visual material and educational instructions.

p.13[2]). However, some portrayals of this story feature Mary conveying Jesus in a sling. An early and magnificent example of this is the Giotto (1266?-1337) fresco illustrated on page 7. The original was painted in 1306, and is in the Arena Chapel in Padua. In some representations of the rest during the flight, Mary is seen with the baby sling loose around her neck. There is even a painting in which not Mary but Joseph is depicted carrying Jesus in the sling. The sight of the father carrying the holy child, especially in a sling, has a dramatic effect. The painter of this image, Frans Francken (1581-1642) apparently wished to emphasise the gruelling nature of the family's journey. The most important conclusion we can draw from these sporadic examples is that Western artists were not entirely unfamiliar with the concept of the baby sling. No more can be said than that. They are so rare that they must be viewed very much as exceptions to the rule. The artists that make use of this attribute probably wished to emphasise that Joseph and Mary were homeless.[3]

This interpretation of the baby sling as a sign of homelessness is supported by the fact that in Western art, beggars, tramps and other itinerants are depicted with all kinds of baby carriers. In our extensive search for images that include baby carriers, we found none that portrayed 'normal' people. We did occasionally come across a print with someone somewhere in a crowd with one or more children on their back, or paintings that featured someone with a baby carrier in a crowd. We quickly concluded, however, that these were never chance figures or passers-by; they were always either poor or homeless. By depicting them with children on the back or neck, the artists apparently wished to suggest that these were people of no fixed abode. Moreover, they could not carry a child in their arms or walk hand-in-hand with them because they needed their hands to be free to carry, to beg, to perform music, or, in the case of gypsies, to read palms.

The oldest depiction of a beggar with a baby carrier that we found came from a missal, or prayer book, from 1323. The beggar is a leper, and the two children in the basket also wear leper's hats. Slings are also frequently to be found in representations of the Seven Acts of Mercy. During the first half of the sixteenth century, the Meester van Alkmaar (Master of Alkmaar) painted people with baby carriers among the hungry and the thirsty. In one case, the child is in a headband, and in another in some kind of sash.[4] In 1528, Lucas van Leyden drew a beggar's family with seven children, two of which were carried in a basket and one at the neck. There is also a striking etching by Rembrandt in 1648 in which a family is portrayed going from house to house begging for alms. The woman carries her youngest child in a sling bound to her back. This frees her hands to hold a stick and receive alms. And finally I would like to mention a nineteenth century drawing we found in the French book, *Curiosités sur les Seins et les Aillements*, written by G.J. Witowski. It features a mother suffering under the weight of her precious burdens: she is nursing an infant in a sling, another child is raiding the provisions from its potty-chair and a child holding her hand is begging.

---

[2] Vogler attempted to describe in detail all the differences between the portrayals of the flight to Egypt. He evidently did not take note of the baby carrier as an attribute. He does not, for example, mention the baby sling when discussing Giotto's Fresco. He does summarise nine depictions of Mary on the donkey with Jesus in swaddling clothes in her arms. We found two representations of the flight to Egypt in the Bible Museum, Amsterdam, in which Mary does indeed wear a baby sling: a 1720 engraving by Bernard Picard in *Figures de la Bible, ws.* (ICONCLASS 73B64.1: 2093B); and a picture after Guido in a printed Bible with 1000 woodcuts prints by D. Broedelet (Amsterdam 1845). And in the Amsterdam National Print Collection *(Rijksprentenkabinet)*: James Johnson after Carle van Loo (1705–1765) (ICONCLASS 73B64.1).

[3] See also the fourteenth century drawing of a group of people including a woman with a child in a sling in George Warner (1912), p. 143–146

[4] There are more examples of such representations. For example, Sheila D. Muller (1985) ill. 52. Joost Cornelis Drooghsloot (1618), ill. 56. Pieter Breughel the Elder (1559) and ill. 63. Jan Steen (1644–48).

All in all, I consider it legitimate to conclude that there is a Western art tradition that associates the carrying of children on the body with beggars, tramps and gypsies. The child carrier thus becomes a symbol of poverty, and this is communicated to the viewer as part of the artist's visual language.[5]

Together with the iconography associated with the flight to Egypt, the depictions of beggars, tramps and gypsies make clear that baby carriers have been known to Western culture since the beginning of the fourteenth century. Although I have found no written evidence of this, it would seem reasonable to assume that they used baby carriers in reality. We do not know however whether they were the only people in Western society to use them. Judging from other visual material we may assume they were. We studied many street scenes, market portraits and farming landscapes, and we found no portrayals of a child in a sling or carrying basket.[6] We were in any case surprised by how few babies featured in representations of outdoor scenes. Was the custom of the time to leave the young ones swaddled at home? If they are to be found they are gener-

---

[5] It is striking that no art historians mention the baby sling or basket as an attribute of poor or itinerant people. Was it, perhaps, too obvious? Alternatively, is it that the sling has no allegorical significance? It is after all, merely an object associated with the poor rather than a metaphor for something else. See L.K. Reinold (1983), P. Vandenbroeck (1987), and the collected works of Sheila D. Muller and Elisabeth Sudeck.

ally either carried loose in an adult's arms, or they are themselves walking. An old woman carrying a child in this way can be seen in a village scene by Joost Cornelis Drooghsloot (1586-1666).[7] Rembrandt made a drawing of a woman with a child on reins wearing a padded hat commonly used to protect the heads of toddlers if they fell. Considering the large numbers of such images, we may presume that children were encouraged to learn to walk as early as possible. This impression is further supported by the fact that young children's clothes often had straps that served as reins.[8] Another revealing image is an eighteenth-century print for children entitled *Huiselijk Bezigheden* (Household Activities). It depicts a mother teaching a child in reins to walk. The caption reads: '*A mother can never rest, as long as her child will not walk.*' Perhaps we should see reins and a protective hat as a Western alternative to the child carrier. The use of baby walkers also suggests it was customary to encourage children to walk as early as possible. These were generally used indoors.[9]

Up to this point, I have mainly discussed seventeenth- and early eighteenth-century portrayals of daily life. The iconographic material is not broadly representative, however. In family portraits, only the social elite appear, and in street, market and farm scenes we see people as the painter would wish us to see them. During the nineteenth and twentieth centuries, the material became more reliable. Artists became increasingly interested in the lives of common people, and photography arrived on the scene. For this reason, it is even more remarkable that we hardly find any evidence of child carriers in the nineteenth century. Mothers either carry the child or hold its hand. Women working the fields sometimes have children around them, but they never carry their child while they work. If necessary, children are laid at the field's edge or on top of a hay cart.[10]

From the middle of the nineteenth century

onwards, photography was also used. Photographers recorded many street scenes. In the Netherlands, for example, these regularly included domestic servants, dressed in white. Sometimes they carry a child or walk hand-in-

---

[6] Only one drawing was found in which a carrier appears that is not directly associated with poverty. It is a village square with three figures: a woman hand-in-hand with a child, and a second child in her back. They are probably on a journey. See the pen drawings by Cornelis Pronk (1691–1759) from the parish of Den Ham (1732. Rijksprentenkabinet, Amsterdam, cat. no. A 2298).

[7] Photograph collection of Arnhem Open Air Museum, AA 112 342, F. 1337-1a J. Slide 11320. See also A. Van der Venne, *Boerenmarkt* (Farmers Market) (1625): a woman walks with a child on her back. Depicted in Christopher Brown (1984), p. 200. See also the painting by Pieter de Bloot (1601–1658) of a lawyer's office (1628), seen in Brown, p. 68: a row of people are queuing politely at the counter, at the rear a woman carries a child on her arms. In the Frans Hals Museum catalogue of 1986 there are several illustrations of young children outdoors (pp. 39, 161, 232, 264)

[8] Cunnington and Buck (3065), p. 129; see also W. Th. Kloek 1977 which includes a portrait of Prince Willem III, aged three or four, in a 'dress' with straps.

[9] For discussion of the iconographic meaning of the baby walker, Simon Schama (1987), pp. 486–92. A splendid depiction by Hieronymous Bosch with Jesus and a walking frame.

The oldest depiction of a beggar with child carrier: a leper with children in a basket on his back. **[Feestmissal 1323. Koninklijke Bibliotheek, Den Haag]**

A beggar woman with a nursing child in a sling around the midriff and a toddler in a seat on her back.
[G.J. Witowski, 1898]

hand with one. In these late nineteenth and early twentieth century photographs, women carrying small children are far more numerous than they are in painted seventeenth century street and market scenes. This suggests, inconclusively, that people began to take their children outside more frequently. Very occasionally, we see domestic servants pushing a pram. It took some time for use of the perambulator to spread from England, where it was invented in 1840[11]. Baby carriers are conspicuously absent from photographic records until the 1970s, during the 'hippy' era. The child carrier was introduced to Western Europe by the consciously 'alternative' culture of this post-war generation.

Nowadays, parents are deluged with advice about how to care for their child, and the first years of a child's life are discussed in minute detail. This stream of specialist childcare manuals began in the late nineteenth century; such literature hardly existed before then. Previously, advice on childcare was passed on by word-of-mouth. The only alternative recourse was to moralists or medical literature. In these works, subjects relating to the care of young children were sometimes discussed. The most important of these topics were feeding, swathing and cradle-rocking. Little further attention was paid to the care of newborn babies in these general advice books.

An example of such a medical advice book is *De Schat der Gesondtheyt*, or 'A Treasury of

Health', written in 1636 by the medical doctor J. van Beverwijck who lived in Dordrecht, in the Netherlands. He advised his readers to leave children alone as much as possible. Only when the child cried for long periods, when teething for example, did he recommend that children be picked up and rocked: 'Excessive agitation caused by riding and rocking is too strong for newborn children.' Van Beverwijck further advised parents not to take children on wagons and boats until the age of three or four.

The physician Stephanus Blankaart is of the same opinion in his 'Discourse on the upbringing and diseases of children': Children have soft brains that 'through rocking may become entirely spoilt, whereby in later years the intellect is dulled and inadequate for proper cogitation'. Fresh air is not good for them because it is too cold in winter and too warm in summer. Blankaart was angered by parents who took their children out on the ice on sledges. He was also exasperated by those who allowed their children to cry, for what use could that possibly serve? From the age of around six months, the child was permitted to crawl around while secured to reins. This he thought better than continually sitting in the potty-chair which caused them to become 'porridge-bags': '[The child] should be active, and if able, walk, as much as possible, in order to grow strong and hardy, for they are continually as if at labour.' In this way a child learns the meaning of work at an early age, claims

---

[10] The impression created by this visual material is confirmed by the meagre written material on the subject. It includes *Onderzoek naar den fabrieksarbeid van gehuwde vrouwen in Nederland* (A study on the factory work of married mothers in the Netherlands) (1911) pp. 184–5. See also W. N. Schilstra (1976), p. 135–6.

[11] See A. Haskell and M. Lewis (1971), p. 74. The 1840 pram, which had three wheels, was intended for older children sitting upright. It was only in the 1880s that prams for babies were produced: a cradle on wheels there could be pushed along. It might seem surprising that nobody had thought of this before. It is not so strange, however, if one considers that the essence of the cradle was that it could be rocked. It was only after objections to rocking had been raised that the idea of a cradle on wheels could be formulated.

Blankaart. At the age of about one year, children may learn to walk – unless they are 'strong and manly', in which case they may begin earlier. A baby walker is altogether unacceptable, in his opinion, as it causes bow-leggedness. And with regard to carrying: 'do not allow it to be performed by older children and young girls because they sometimes allow the child to fall backwards, and this can lead to lameness in later life.'

More than a century later, the clergymen and pedagogue J.F. Martinet published his *Handbook for Fatherland Families*. Some new ideas are to be found here. He is ill-disposed

towards the habit of keeping children at home in stuffy dark rooms, and he encourages parents to take their children outside and ensure that they get sufficient fresh air – although he advises caution with strong light. He discourages carrying children in one's arms for fear that it may cause the child to grow 'crooked'. Furthermore, a child could be made lame by an unexpected movement. 'In general, I consider the carrying of a child on the arm to be damaging or, at least, dangerous, especially by less attentive women.' By 'women' he means wet nurses or nannies, who used to carry the child on the left arm in order to keep their right hand free. Martinet preferred them to use a trailer, 'which provides a beneficial rocking motion'. Reins, however, are strongly discouraged. He argues that a child should be allowed to crawl until it stands up by itself. Much of this sounds reasonably modern, which makes the reasoning behind his opinion that children should choose the time to walk themselves all the more curious: 'In this way, they will learn not to place the foot straight forwards, but rather turned outwards at an angle, which gives a more surefooted gait.'

In the nineteenth century, the fear that children could be spoiled began to prevail among pedagogues. A clear example of this is Dr. S. Bruining's discourse on baby care published in 1865, 'Feeding, Care and Death in the First Year of Life.' In it, he describes the rocking, carrying and wheeling around of children as forms of unnecessary comfort. A similar tone is maintained in the frequently reprinted 'Handbook for Mothers'. It was written by G.A.N Allebé and published in 1845; the eighth edition appeared in 1908. Allebé considers rocking the cradle to be 'damaging and unnecessary'. It is better to remove the cause of restlessness. Furthermore, continual rocking leads to sleep becoming a form of intoxication. Allebé considers it more useful to do away with the cradle completely. He is,

Left: a beggar family. The woman carries a child in a bag on her back.
[Etching by Rembrandt, 1648. Rijksmuseum, Amsterdam]

A soldier's widow with a child in her back.
[Oil painting by Cornelia Sheffer-Lammer, 1769–1813]

due to the modernisation of prams, which by then had handles on each side. The use of the modern pram was no longer controversial. This is further demonstrated by a Dutch Reformational handbook for clothing, published in 1909, in which the *wickelbett* is recommended, not in order to take the child outside (for as everyone knows 'small children are rarely carried in this country nowadays') but because it was useful when parents wished to transfer the child from the bed to the pram.

In essence, the advice given to young mothers at the beginning of the twentieth century by authoritative paediatricians such as Cornelia de Lange was this: cradle-rocking is bad for brains and bowels, fresh air is good, and the premature use of aids such as baby walkers and harnesses is damaging. If necessary, use a playpen. To carry a child on one arm will harm it, and is therefore proscribed. If the child must be carried, one must alternate the arm used. The pram is acceptable and may also be used as a cradle – as long as it is not continually rocked backwards and forwards.

Only in 1927 did rocking cradles come to be seen in a more positive light. In an oratory, Doctor de Lange reviewed her earlier stance on the matter: '*The rocking cradle, how we have reviled it, and how gladly I would sometimes welcome its return! How fearful we have been of overindulging. The cradle may be old-fashioned but it provides warmth and protection, and that is required by some sensitive children.*' In *Moederschapzorg* (Motherhood Care), a Catholic periodical published by the training school for midwives in Heerlen, this renewed enthusiasm for the cradle was promptly endorsed in a special article on the subject. The author claims that to lull a child into sleep with lullabies while rocking its cradle is a universal phenomenon. Moreover, the Western idea that it could be harmful is purely theoretical; we don't know what the child wants. Among 'wild peoples', mothers do not even have cradles and they always have their children on their backs, moving with

however a staunch advocate of fresh air. He advises mothers to take their child outside every day or put its bed on the balcony or in the garden. In this context, Allebé believes the German *wickelbett* to be a useful invention. The *wickelbett* was a cushion with straps into which a baby could be safely secured and then carried. He nonetheless considered carrying a baby on the arm to be the best option, as long as the arm is alternated. If this is not done, the baby's spine could become deformed. He could see no advantage to the use of baby walkers, because a child learns to walk when it is ready. Allebé remains sceptical regarding the use of prams: he is of the opinion that children cannot lie comfortably in them, can see very little and tend to get the wind in their faces. But in the 1908 edition, he withdrew his objections them. The author also objects to the manner in which Western mothers of the time used medical arguments to justify their attitudes; he considers it merely a means by which they can avoid their maternal responsibilities.

Despite these enlightened voices, fear of over-indulgence prevailed and set the tone in advice for mothers; 'messing around' with crying children was strongly discouraged. It was thought more important to leave the child alone. We found an apposite illustration of this general opinion in the 1935 *Encyclopedie voor Moeders* (Encyclopaedia for Mothers). It was explained that a portable cradle can be useful when taking a child in a car, but that portable cradles, as were used in olden times and still encountered among 'travelling people', were a symptom of unrest and therefore bad. Children need their own, stationary, place.

Modern fatherhood in the 1970s.
[Photograph Hans and Laura Samson]

Not until the 1950s did the tide begin to turn. In 1955, Zwitsal, a company manufacturing childcare products, produced a book entitled *Moeder Worden* (Becoming a Mother). In one passage, the reader is encouraged to show understanding for babies that cry because they are alone all day in their bed or pram. Elsewhere, customs of 'primitive' peoples are described. For example, baby's experience close physical contact with their mother throughout the day, and these children cry less. However, the author does not conclude that Western mothers should also use baby slings, although they should pick up and carry their children if necessary. The most widely read pedagogue since the 1950s, Doctor Benjamin Spock, seems to be recommending the use of slings somewhat cryptically when in his 1965 book he emphasises the child's need for fresh air, pointing out that there are many different ways to transport a child by carrying it on the back or side.

We find the first explicit positively worded mention of a child carrier in a 1972 edition of the magazine *Ouders van Nu* (Modern Parents). The subject is a seat for hanging on one's back. It is recommended for holidays and long walks. Perhaps surprisingly, the accompanying illustration features the father rather than the mother carrying it. The carry-seat is clearly not intended for daily use. It is an additional accessory to be used when travelling. In the ensuing years, further articles about new designs appeared in the publication with increasing frequency. In 1974, the magazine introduced its own baby sling under the name *Easy Rider*. The Dutch women's magazine *Margriet* printed a pattern for a sling – to be made of denim.

It is striking that in these early years, baby carriers were praised for their practical advantages. It is easier to manoeuvre than a cumbersome pram; the parent's hands are free and the child can see the world around it. As the pedagogue H. Jolly writes on the subject of the

carry-seat in his *Kinderverzorging en Opvoeding* (Child Care and Parenting): '*No one who is used to this method of carrying, which is extremely practical in busy shops, needs to be concerned by disapproving looks from members of the older generation. The child is enjoying the view high on its father or mother's back, and it is by no means bad for its own back.*' He does, though, advise the use of a pram for longer journeys. Children enjoy being pushed and it is warmer. Jolly argues that children should not be continually carried. It may be the case that African babies cry less, but he still prefers the child seat on which it can sit at the table with its mother. He believes that excessive crying is due to a lack of social rather than physical contact.

Only at the end of the 1980s are the emotional benefits of child carriers emphasised. The general tone has changed and now babies are seen to experience a naturally intimate physical contact with their parents simply by being carried in a sling. The natural rocking motion settles them. In an article in a 1992 edition of *Ouders van Nu* entitled 'All Babies Cry, But Why?', loneliness is one of the causes discussed. '*For some babies, the transition from a safe and warm womb to a cradle or bed is an enormous one. When alone, they feel ill-at-ease and cry until they feel physical contact again with their mother or father... keep your baby close to you or carry it in a sling*'

Nonetheless, the child carrier remained a contentious issue. The 1992 *Consumentengids* (Consumer Guide) states: '*A baby carry-bag or carry-seat is fine as an extra, but you cannot walk around with one for hours on end. It is far easier to put your child in a pram or pushchair.*' It is difficult to predict how attitudes towards the baby carrier will develop. But from the preceding passages one infers that they have only recently become established in Western culture. Only in the early 1970s was this object, which had been associated with paupers for centuries, transformed into a childcare acces-

sory for unconventional parents who were unperturbed by the surprised and often disapproving stares from onlookers.

Nowadays, one can buy many aids for carrying children. There are many variations on the carry-seat as a standalone accessory or in combination with a frame for a pram or car seat. A variety of slings is also available. In general, baby carriers worn on the back are intended for travelling substantial distances, and advertisements for them usually feature men; their design is becoming more ingenious. Carriers worn on the front, however, are usually worn by women (if advertisers are to be believed), feature fewer gadgets and resemble simpler traditional slings. Thus, baby carriers are an example of Western and non-Western traditions blending in fascinating ways.

Chapter 2.3.1

North America

Rockin' the cradle: childcare among Native North Americans

A.R. Lith[1]

Almost all Native North Americans spend the first years of their lives swaddled in a baby carrier. This is a surprising common characteristic among otherwise widely disparate cultures. The swaddling and carrying of papooses (infants) occurred throughout the continent. The methods and means of carrying, however, varied according to local custom.

The infant was carried from a few days after birth until around the age it learnt to walk. Baby carriers would be seen everywhere: on a mothers back, attached to a *travois* (a method of transport consisting of two long poles, usually dragged behind a horse), swinging in a tipi or simply leant against something. The mother or another member of the family was always around, so the baby was never alone. The carrier generally consisted of several components that each had their own function. A framework formed the basis of the construction. The bag in which the baby lay was sometimes integrated into the frame, and sometimes detachable from it. The soft lining of the bag made it a pleasant environment for the infant. The carrier protected the child against undesirable external influences; amulets and fetishes hung from the frame. The baby was both safe and easily manoeuvrable.

Native North Americans paid much attention to the care and upbringing of their children. The carrier was beautifully decorated. The beads and dentalium (tooth) shells required for decoration were very costly and often only available by trade. Animal hides would be bartered for beads – symbols of wealth and prestige.

Mothers generally took care of their own children. They would leave them in the charge of others for a few hours at the most. Consequently, mothers with very young children hardly left the camp, and never walked long distances. European observers were surprised to see that even somewhat older children were carried in the arms of their fearsome warrior fathers.

Fathers played an important role in the upbringing of children. If a child were sick, a father would call upon supernatural forces to encourage recovery. Older boys were prepared for adult life by their fathers. Native Americans lived in a frequently hostile and unpredictable environment inhabited by spirits. Existence was harsh and they suffered many privations. Child mortality was high. In some regions of North America it was often difficult to find sufficient food during the long winters.

[1] This article was based on research materials made available by P. Hovens and L-Krosenbrink Gelissen. The publisher would like to thank the researchers.

At the end of the nineteenth century, Otis T. Mason, of the United States National Museum, enumerated the many functions that carry-cots, baby slings and cradles had among the original inhabitants of North America. They used them as warm and safe beds in which infants could sleep, whether lying or standing. They also served as a method of transport whereby they were carried on the mothers back with the help of a forehead strap. Furthermore, the carry-cot indicated a family's social

Ojibwa babies by a bark tipi in the Indian village at Earls Court, London. This photograph was taken during an exhibition, and was distributed as a postcard.
[Photograph Gale and Polden Ltd., c. 1900. World Arts Museum, Rotterdam]

rank. Baby carriers also had a part to play in religious traditions: the outgrowing of the cradle, for example, was an aspect of the transition ritual leading to the next phase of life.

Carry-cots were constructed in such a way that women could take them along when performing a variety of tasks. The colours and movement, and the sounds made by the ornaments, all kept the child occupied until it fell asleep.

More recently, Rosemary Lessard, of the Chandler Institute in Santa Fe, has described a number of other functions of baby carriers. She pointed out that the construction and decorations of the carrier indicated ethnic identity. They also strengthened mutual relationships. If it were made by someone other than the mother, they would receive a gift, such as a horse, as a sign of gratitude. The family's prestige was indicated by the quality of the baby carrier. Moreover, the decorations were creative expressions – an art form.

The baby remained tightly wrapped in the carrier for the first year of its life. Babies were generally not left to cry, and their demands were quickly met. It was thought that in this way, children would learn to dominate their environment, and that independence and self-confidence – important qualities for important positions of leadership – would be stimulated. This was not true for all tribes however. Cheyenne children were taught not to cry. The Cheyenne were belligerent warriors and feared that the noise of crying children might betray their location. If the baby continued crying after all its needs had been met, it was wrapped and placed in the carry-cot, which was hung from the branch of a tree until it stopped. In this way the child came to understand that crying was useless.

Because of the enormous cultural diversity it is difficult to describe the indigenous cultures of North America in general terms. Population groups adapted to their natural environment. The material culture reflected the flora and fauna of the region. Baby carriers were made in a variety of ways. Nature provided all materials required for childcare: wood for the frame, animal skins to keep the child warm, cane from which the basket was fashioned, moss that served as nappies and porcupine quills for decoration. These materials had spiritual as well as practical significance. They believed that all living things –

plants and animals as well as human beings – had souls. Baby carriers were more than mere objects; they embodied the power of the spirits of the materials.

The form and appearance of the baby carrier were largely dependent on what nature had to offer locally. They were also affected by living conditions. The Inuit, living in the **arctic circle**, depended for survival on the whales and fish they caught, and lived in permanent settlements. Other groups led a nomadic existence hunting caribou. The Inuit had their own method of carrying babies: nursing infants were usually carried in the mother's parka, which was widened for the purpose. The child was also strapped tightly against the mother. Children's clothing was made from animal hide.

Indigenous peoples living south of the Inuit, in the **subarctic region**, adopted the widened parka for women as a means of transporting children. Inhabitants of this region often lived semi-nomadic lives. They lived from catching fish and hunting small game. A number of population groups in the Athapaskan-speaking region also made carry-cots from birch bark. Three pieces were sewn together forming a base, top and hood. Willow stakes and broad strips of birch ensured that the structure was stable. The baby was wrapped in furs and laid in the carrier to be secured with strips of leather. Beaded decorations were applied to the hood, which protected against the swarms of mosquitoes frequently encountered in the region. An animal skin filled with moss was used to soak up the urine. The baby only had an opportunity to move when the moss was being replaced.

The Kaska live in an environment with no birch, and therefore made no baby carriers. During cold weather, they wrapped their babies in clean blankets such that their legs lay straight next to each other. As it became warmer the baby's hands were left uncovered and the blanket was placed loosely over the sleeping child's face. The swaddled infant was placed in a reindeer skin bag containing a layer of moss. The mother carried the bag – without shoulder straps. At the age of a few months, the blanket was replaced by clothing resembling a Western romper suit: an overall or long shirt with a warm undershirt. Sometimes, a bag was used to carry the child rather than a baby sling, and this would also contain provisions. In this case, the child hung with its face turned towards its mother. From the sixth month, the parent carried the infants on an arm or hip. A long shawl was sometimes tied around the parent's shoulder and the child to provide support at the hip.

The Tahltan wrapped their infants in rabbit skins and placed them in a fur sling or carry-bag. Here too, moss was used to take up the child's waste. They did not use wood, bark or wickerwork for their baby carriers; they were fashioned from large pieces of tanned caribou or moose leather. At home it was unfolded and used as an eiderdown. The swaddled child was secured to the carrier with strips of leather. The ends of the skin were folded double and tied over the child's legs. The upper part of the skin was sometimes narrowed to create a protective hood for the child's head. On the back of the carrier were leather loops that enabled the mother to carry the child with its back against hers. As a rule, a carrier was made for each child. While being wrapped, the baby's legs received particular attention: the Tahltan wanted their children to be strong walkers. They scarcely decorated the carriers. Some edges or seams of the skin were perforated. Later, however, blue or red piping was applied to the seams.

Salmon was the main food in the **north-western coastal region**, but berries were also collected. The indigenous population lived in large wooden houses, and they were renowned wood carvers. The Kwakiutl made child carriers

Mescalero Apache woman with her child, New Mexico.
[Photograph G.B. Whittick, 1883–6. World Arts Museum, Rotterdam]

from planks. The interior was made more comfortable with small strips of cedar bark, and the exterior was decorated with painted or carved family symbols. In this way, social rank was emphasised. If the mother was occupied, the carrier was hung from a branch. The mother would rock it to and fro by pulling on a rope attached to it. Large ceremonial baby carriers were used during namegiving ceremonies. These were hung on long stakes in front of the house. Four shamans performed the ceremony. They would sit at the four corners of the cradle, shake their rattles and speak out the name of the child.

It was customary among many tribes living on the north-western coast to flatten their heads artificially. In order to achieve this, a piece of bark or wood was attached to the top of the baby carrier and then over the infant's skull and secured to the frame with straps. This continued until the child was about one year old. The forehead was flattened by this procedure and the skull was distinctly egg-shaped when viewed from the side. This was considered a beautification.

The Makah and the Chinook fashioned baby carriers in the form of a canoe from cedar and alder wood. Infants were wrapped in hides or cedar-fibre mats and laid in the carrier on a layer of torn-off strips of cedar bark. A handle was cut into the bottom of the carrier, but its purpose is unclear. The choice of a canoe form for the carrier is probably related to the custom of placing deceased infants on a river or lake to be taken with the current to the realm of the spirits.

The Tlingit made their baby carrier and began collecting the tree moss they required for it before the child arrived. A straight back was considered important for Tlingit adults, and the carriers were therefore made of robust material. While the mother was busy with her daily tasks, the carrier was leant against a sturdy support. Indoors, the baby slept in a hammock or a swing made of a blanket or sealskin. The mother could make this swing by pulling on a length of rope. When the mother had to work outside, the baby accompanied her: the cot was carried in a fold in the blanket that the mother wore on her back, and kept in place by a rope around her midriff. This resulted in the child lying more or less diagonally across her back, and the baby being able to look over her shoulder. Fathers, grandparents and other relatives carried children in the same way. The carrier was not secured with straps, so the mother could easily nurse the child. At the age of four months, a larger carrier was used, which offered the child more freedom of movement.

Indigenous **Californians** made beautiful baskets. They ate mashed acorns supplemented with berries, game and fish. The Pomo and the Wintun made mainly twined basketwork. Their baby carriers were oval, rectangular or V-shaped. Some had wickerwork seats, the side of which were sharply curved allowing freedom of movement for the baby's legs. The baby was carried in a seated position. Plaited leather hoods were attached to the carrier to protect the child from insects and the sun. Sometimes, carriers for boys and girls were painted differently. The Yokut, for example, applied diagonal lines to the hood of a boy's carrier and zigzag patterns to a girl's. Depending on the mother's activity, the carrier would be leant against something secure or carried on the mother's back. It was sometimes placed in a hole on the ground. Many coloured objects hung from the cot – they distracted the child but also had spiritual significance. Mothers made miniature carriers as toys that helped prepare their daughters for motherhood. Girls played with the smallest ones and carried larger ones on the back.

The **south-west** was inhabited mainly by farmers, such as the Hopi and the Zuñi, and by the nomadic peoples, the Navajo and Jicarilla

Apache, for example. Their primary source of nutrition was maize. Baby carriers were usually made from a single piece of hardwood bent into a U-shape and held in place by wooden crosspieces, which resulted in a horseshoe shape. Infants were swaddled in animal hides, laid on a layer of willow bark and secured with straps. Jicarilla Apaches wrapped their newborns in buffalo or puma hides. The fur on the inside created a warm and comfortable environment for the infant. The Jicarilla only wrapped their young from the age of two months, since it was thought irresponsible to straighten the legs before the navel had healed. The child was no longer wrapped if it indicated its discomfort by crying. Carriers were made immediately after birth, sometimes by the mother but usually by older women. There was a purifying ritual involving the scattering of pollen over the carrier. It was decorated with the bones and legs of turkeys to provide protection against evil spirits and to ensure good health. The quilt of animal skin was usually decorated with beads. The carrier was sufficiently large that a child could remain in it until it could walk.

Among the Yuman-speaking Plateau peoples, the carrier was fashioned by either the child's mother or maternal grandmother. The sides of the oval frame were almost parallel, and the open space was filled with woven willow twigs. The frame itself was made from branches bent into U-shapes. These were bound together with rope and buried for a time in damp earth so they would maintain their shape. The carrier was then covered liberally with pitch. It was then clad in a woven Hopi blanket onto which softened cedar bark was laid. The baby was swaddled with its arms against its body and placed in the carrier. It was then covered by more bark and then firmly wrapped in a blanket. The usually broad carrying strap was sometimes made from a band woven by the Hopi or Navajo. The carrier also had a hood woven from approximately 40 reed stems. If it remained

undamaged, it was passed on to another child.

The River Yuman, who lived along the Colorado River, also made the carrier before the baby was born. The frame was fashioned from a rather narrow plank of wood, which was arched at the top, with long straight sides. Sticks were secured crosswise and a broad wickerwork basket was woven onto it. The gender of the child was indicated by the decoration on the hood and in the weaving pattern of the straps that held the basket to the frame. The carrier could be used a number of times within the family, but it was never passed over to other families. When the child outgrew the carrier after three months or so, a similar but larger version was made. In contrast to the custom among most other tribes, River Yuman allowed their babies to cry. This was considered good for the child's development.

The **Great Basin**, the vast desert plateau around the Great Salt Lake, was inhabited by the Paiute, Shoshoni and the Utes, among others. They led a nomadic existence, continually moving on in search of food. The Northern Utes made various types of baby carriers. The most prevalent was one made by bending a willow branch into an oval shape. Vertical willow slats were secured to this brace, and small pieces of bark were woven between them. The frame was then pushed into an envelope of buffalo skin and sewn shut. Carriers usually had a hood made of rawhide or willow wickerwork. Boy's carriers usually had an opening for the penis and girls' carriers had an opening for the strips of birch bark that were placed between their legs to absorb urine. This older design was usually not decorated.

The most simple baby carriers comprised an animal skin in which the baby was swaddled and then strapped into place. Two sticks passed through holes in the sides and these were attached to the forehead straps that the mother used to support the carrier on her back. This design included a hood identical to the one mentioned above. A third design was made from a pine plank. A bag made of animal hide was attached to the plank with leather straps that passed through holes at its edges. These carriers were often decorated with beads, leather strips and paint. Boys' carriers were painted white, and girls', yellow.

The **Inland Plateau** is a diversified region with abundant food sources. Inhabitants lived by hunting buffalo and deer, gathering tubers and berries, and fishing. Groups that hunted were nomadic, and farmers lived in houses that were partly underground. The Salish, living in the northern part of the Inland Plateau, made their baby carriers from wickerwork. Any desired shape could be created for the carrier by selecting different lengths of slender slats that were secured to each other with the roots of cedar trees. The interwoven reeds were decorated with coloured strips of bark.

The Modoc made egg-shaped baby carriers of twined willow or tule wickerwork. The inside was clad in deer or rabbit fur. The carrier was made only after the birth of the child, because it was believed that the baby would otherwise be stillborn. The newborn child was not wrapped. Its first carrier was usually fashioned from tule by a female member of the family because it was easily twined and thus quickly completed. When the mother was up to strength again she made a sturdier object using willow osiers. This was used until the child could walk. After use, the carrier was burned; each baby had its own carrier made specially for it. These carry-cots were generally carried on the left arm with the child facing outwards and a strap around the mother's shoulder. Sometimes it was carried on the mother's back with a supporting strap around her forehead. Salish mothers made their carriers immediately after the birth of their children. The age at which the baby was first put into the carrier varied between ten days and a month. Until that time, it was wrapped in animal skins and

sometimes placed in a bag. The baby sling was made from deerskin. The frame onto which it was hung was of cedar wood, or, if this could not be afforded, pine. It was slightly ovoid – the lower end was narrowest. Later designs were covered with buffalo hide. Holes were drilled along the edges for the ropes that held the frame in shape, and also a bag in place. There was a handle on the carrier. During a journey it was carried on the back with the aid

White Mountain Apache women in south-eastern Arizona, with water jug and baby carrier, 1883.
[Photograph C. Duhem, commissioned by H. ten Kate, Ten Kate Photograph collection. National Museum of Ethnology, Leiden]

of a forehead strap. On each occasion that the baby was wrapped, it was massaged. It was also powdered, and aromatic flowers were placed with it in the carrier to make it smell pleasant and grow healthy and strong.

The Salish word for 'flathead' also meant 'free'. A flat stone or other flat object was placed on the heads of Salish infants and secured with straps. The baby was then wrapped. Children of slaves, however, did not receive this 'beauty' treatment. The carriers were originally much shorter than those observed and described by ethnographers. It is therefore assumed that the flattening of the head was not a tradi-

tional characteristic of the Salish as it was of the Coeur d'Alene. It is not known when the Salish adopted this practice.

On the **Plains**, the vast prairies at the heart of North America, the buffalo hunt was the most important source of income until the Europeans arrived. A variety of baby carriers was made in this part of the country. The cot made by the Kiowa was characteristic of the region and was later used by the Comanche, the Cheyenne and the Dakota. This comprised two pointed slats attached to each other by a connecting piece, forming a sturdy V–shape. An upper crosspiece was affixed two-thirds of the way up. A leather bag shaped like a shoe was attached to this frame. A simpler variant of this design comprised an animal-skin bag attached to a frame of thin slats.

Bead and porcupine-needle decorations were usually applied to the entire surface area of the leather bag. One could deduce the parentage of the child from these decorations. The Lakota, for example, had red leather bags decorated with needles and white beadwork. Decorations made with beads displaced those made with needles because they were easier to make.

Decorations also had symbolic meaning. The decorations on Cheyenne and Arapaho slings were made by a secret society of quill workers. This was an association of women who applied porcupine needle decorations to which protective, health-giving and life-perpetuating properties were ascribed. The baby carriers were made under the supervision of one of the members of the society. Arapaho carriers were decorated with the plaited rosettes illustrated on pages XX and XX. Most were round; others were square or trapezoid. These were fixed to separate pieces of leather that were, in turn, sewn onto the hood. It was sometimes possible to see if the carrier had been made for a boy or girl: horses were associated with boys, for example. Baby carriers

Paiutes children in the Colorado Valley, Utah, 1874.
[Photograph E.O. Beaman/ J.K. Hillers. World Arts Museum, Rotterdam]

were presented as gifts to the mother by family members or non-family members. At least one case is known of one mother receiving 22 baby carriers on the birth of her child.

The Prairie-dwelling Bungi, or Ojibwa, made baby carriers from animal skins folded lengthways to create a bag. The baby was held in place using leather laces. Moss bags decorated with beads were often hung on a boy's clothes during the performance of a grass dance. This dance, which could only be carried out by the grass warrior's society, was viewed as a rite of passage to adulthood and as a warrior's dance of honour. The baby carriers were sometimes attached to wooden frames, but were also carried loose. The baby's head was protected by a wooden arch projecting upwards from the frame. Women carried them on the back, supported by straps around the forehead and shoulders.

The Blood, or Blackfoot, fashioned their baby carriers from willow twigs. Originally, these were bent, stretched and fastened horizontally. They were later sawn from a large sheet of wood and covered with buffalo hide. The section around the head was often decorated with beads and flower motifs. The infant was firmly strapped into an elongated bag that formed part of the buffalo hide covering. The bag had a hood that was fastened around the baby's head. Some carriers were lined with fur, while others were decorated with hanging leather strips that covered the lacing, or with long bead or shell necklaces.

The baby was carried on the mother's back, the carrier held in place by shoulder straps. Alternatively, it was hung from the pommel on the mother's saddle. Blood baby carriers had no wooden projection protecting the child's face. The carriers were originally covered with buffalo hide, but when the buffalo were all but extinct, this was replaced by muslin or canvas. Except among the Cheyenne and the Arapaho Porcupine, beads gradually replaced needle decorations. The needles had a religious sig-

nificance to these tribes. There was a resurgence in the use of porcupine needles during the First World War because insufficient beads could be imported from Europe. Thereafter, the making of traditional baby carriers gradually decreased. Western cradles displaced them.

The **northeast** is home to many different cultures. A distinction is made between the Iroquois and Algonquin, who farmed, and the peoples of the Great Lakes, who lived a semi-nomadic existence. Among the latter, the baby carrier consisted of rectangular planks with a layer of vegetable matter into which the baby was laid and then secured with strips of leather. It also often had a foot support. At the upper end of the plank, a U-shaped piece of wood was attached to prevent any damage to the child's head. The animal skins were often decorated with porcupine needles. The design was generally sober and functional, though some baby carriers did have decorations carved into the wooden top section.

Iroquois baby carriers were convenient for the mother but did not guarantee correct positioning of the infant. The baby was wrapped and fixed to the framework with beadwork straps that covered his entire body except for his face. The carrier was richly decorated with carvings, silver, paint or other woods. The carrying strap that encircled the carrier also went around the mother's forehead.

Food, safety and survival were primary concerns in the first year of life. Because child mortality was high, the birth ceremony was often postponed until the first birthday. It is not without good reason that in many indigenous tribes continued carrying and swaddling until the child could walk. This often roughly coincided with the first birthday. The way indigenous people treated their children is a clear indicator of their attitudes towards personality development. Only after the child could walk was its acculturation, or participation in its community, initiated. During the period in which the child was swaddled, the emphasis was on aspects of personality development rather than the acquisition of social skills. In other words, during the first year it was important to stimulate those traits that would enable it to survive as an adult. The main carer, the mother, ensured that no physical harm came to the child in its first year. Only if it indeed managed to survive that year was it considered worthwhile to teach him how to become a valued member of the community.

With the gradual disappearance of the original Native American material culture, and its replacement by industrially manufactured Western goods, traditional baby carriers, baby bags and cradles also disappeared. However, the implements required to swaddle and carry babies are again being made by native craftsmen as a means of confirming cultural identity and as a mark of pride in the heritage of the original inhabitants of North America. These objects are finding a ready market among tourists, and their production is increasing.

A Peruvian baby in swaddled on a sling. As soon as the mother can work again, she wraps the child in napkins and binds these with a belt. She then lies the child on a blanket or piece of sheepskin on the sling. The corners are folded over the baby, and the whole package is swung carefully over her shoulder. The two loose ends are bound tightly in front of the chest.
[All photographs in this chapter by E. van der Hoeven]

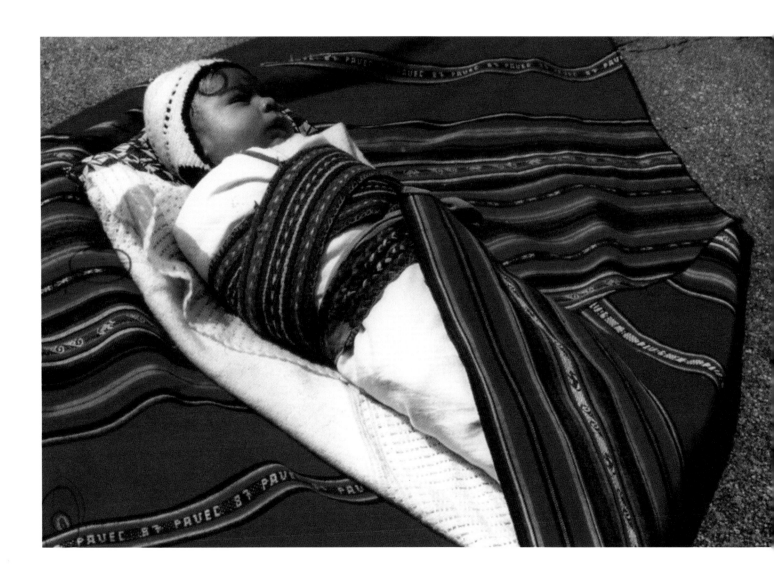

Chapter 2.3.2

South America/ Andes

Travelling safely with an infant

E. van der Hoeven

In both rural and urban areas of the South American Andean countries of Ecuador, Peru and Bolivia, one sees the familiar and characteristic sight of women walking with a colourful cargo on their back. It is the *manta*, *q'epiña*, *q'eperina* or *lliklla*, a hand-woven cloth in which the woman transports her wares for market or things she needs for the journey. But often the contents move and produce sounds – it is her child.

For women living in the Andes region of southern Peru – between Cusco and Lake Titicaca – life is hard. Their responsibilities are many and varied. A woman must take care of and feed her youngest baby while performing these tasks, usually outside. Only in emergencies can she call on the assistance of a sister or her mother.

In a region where for centuries people have carried loads on their backs, where there are no day nurseries, where prams are either impractical or an unattainable luxury, and where a woman must be close to her child in order to care for it and feed it, a baby sling is the most obvious solution. Women usually weave two baby slings before the birth of their first child. In cities one can now buy them ready-made. The mother will use them in turn, keeping the most beautiful for visits to the market or church, or for parties. As long as they are in good repair, she will continue to use them for subsequent children. When they are worn out, they are used around the house. When they are no longer of any use, they are burned.

As soon as the mother can work after giving birth, she swaddles her baby with nappies and belts, and wraps it in the sling. This precludes the possibility of the baby's limbs being caught or twisted as the mother moves around. The infant's head rests on a piece of sheepskin or on a cushion. The inhabitants of the Andes believe that swaddling encourages the bones to grow and become sturdy.

When the mother wishes to feed the child, she shifts the entire bundle to the front and opens the cloth. The baby lies comfortably at the breast without changing position. The child is always close by and the mother can soothe it whenever necessary. If it cries when it is on the mother's back, she can move her body to and fro and tap her hands on the underside of the *q'epiña* to calm it.

When the arms and legs are somewhat stronger, at the age of five or six months, the baby takes on a more vertical position. Between its first and second birthday, it will sit. Even after the child can walk, situations may arise where it has to be carried – when ill, for example. When a new baby is born, care of very young children is temporarily taken over either by the grandmother or an older (at least eight-year-old) sister. From six months the baby wears regular clothes: vest, long woollen trousers, jumper and hat. From the moment it can walk and sit up straight in the carrier, is no longer needs the sheepskin.

In the past – as it still is today in isolated regions – it was customary to rub medicinal herbs into the entire body of women who had recently given birth. The sling that she had woven for her baby was then wrapped around her, in the belief that this would facilitate a quick recovery after delivery. In some areas, the mother actually lies on the sling so that it receives all the forces emanating from the womb during birth. These forces then protect the newborn child for a period. On the island of Taquile, newborn babies are wrapped in the *q'epiña* for the first few days after birth and laid next to the mother. Both are shaded from the sun by a reed mat, because its rays can cause injury or illness.

The baby sling also plays a role during certain celebrations. On All Souls Day and All Saints Day, young girls living in the Cusco region receive a doll made of bread dough from their mothers. The children wrap the doll in a small sling and walk about with it proudly. And during traditional marriage celebrations in some areas, guests are given a *q'epiña* with a doll inside it. Guests then dance with the bride while wearing this tied on their backs.

The *q'epiña* does not play such an important symbolic role everywhere, but even in urban areas, the sling is strongly associated with babies. When a woman was asked where her carrying cloth was, she said that she had none. When asked why not she said, 'Because I have no child.'

Girls living in the Andes quickly become accustomed to the *q'epiña* as part of their clothing. Even a girl who is sometimes carried in one herself will look on with interest as her mother wraps a younger brother or sister in the *q'epiña*. She then imitates the procedure with her dolls. The carrying cloth is the ultimate symbol of womanhood. Men in the Andes never carry babies, as they would feel ashamed to do so. It could imply that a man's

wife has left him and he as been unable to find any female family members willing to help him.

People travel a lot in the Andes. They visit local markets, marriages, harvest celebrations and fertility rituals for cattle. A mother likes to travel with her newborn child because it is still an angel that will protect her from all malign spirits she may encounter on the journey. Weaving a *q'epiña* is heavy and precise work. The textile craft is closely linked with all aspects of life in the Andes. For this reason, it is important for a girl to learn to weave. She watches her mother working at the loom from a very young age, and helps with tightening

Woman sowing with her grandson on her back; San Pedro, Cusco, Peru.

threads and other tasks. The better a girl can weave, the more she is appreciated. Traditionally, a young man chooses his bride according to the beauty and quality of her weaving.

When making a woven fabric, the woman chooses the figures, or *pallays*, she prefers. She is, however, somewhat limited in their choice. It may traditionally be the case that in her village or region certain *pallays* must, or must not, be used. In the region around the city of Cusco, for example, one sees woven into fabrics motifs of horses, flags and men with hats. These designs commemorate the native freedom fighter Tupac Amaru III, who was quartered in Cusco by the Spanish in 1781. In the area around Lake Titicaca, many fish, birds and snake figures are woven. In farming cultures, stylised plant and animal motifs prevail, such as flowers, corncobs, lama footprints and fields. Some *pallays* are not region-specific,

On All Souls' Day and All Saints Day, little girls in Cusco and the surrounding area are given a doll made of bread dough by their mother. They wrap the doll in a small sling and walk around proudly with it.

and these are in more general use. These include: *Inti*, the sun; *quenqo*, channel; *qocha*, lagoon; and *qoyllur*, star (see also pages 147-149). *Pallays* originally had symbolic meanings, and a weaver could use certain *pallays* to communicate a message that people in her community would understand. In modern times, knowledge of these meanings has either diminished or vanished, and *pallays* are only used for decorative purposes. An exception can be found on the island of Taquile, where craftswoman still weave an 'annual report' into belts using a different *pallay* for each important event in the family.

Colour choice and colour combinations are also bound up with local traditions. Puno custom, for example, dictates that juxtaposed colours should not contrast too strongly with each other, as this could bring about misfortune. A neutralising colour is therefore woven between such colours, which creates a rainbow effect. In the valleys northeast of Cusco, red white and black predominate. In the Piumarca district, five, six or seven colours are used: pink, red, yellow, orange, blue, green and purple. According to tradition *pallays* and colours are chosen according to their symbolic meaning. This tradition is also disappearing, and colours are generally chosen according to personal taste from within the range of local tradition.

Chapter 2.3.3

South America/ Amazon

A token of skill

A. Bant

Tsompirontsi. *Illustrations of the motifs on the bones can be found on pages 84-85.*

The Ashaninka live in a number of great Peruvian river basins and on the eastern slopes of the Andes. With a population of around 20,000 they form the largest tribal society in the Peruvian Amazon. Ashaninka women carry their babies against their upper midriff. A girl will carry her younger brothers and sisters if she has any, and if she does not her mother will knot a sheet around her containing a large cassava. In this way, a daughter prepares herself for her future tasks. An Ashaninka baby carrier is called a *tsompirontsi*.

The location of the original Ashaninka territory – reasonably accessible by land from the coast – and its temperate tropical climate meant that they were visited by missionaries as early as the sixteenth century. These mission workers probably introduced the *cushma*, the garment traditionally worn by the Ashaninka. Although most Ashaninka wear western clothing nowadays, the *cushma* is preferred for official occasions.

The *cushma* is made by sewing together at the seams two equally-sized rectangles of woven cotton. Woven tree-bark fibre was also used in the past. In recent times, *cushmas* for women and children are sometimes made from machine-produced cloth rather than hand-woven material. Children's *cushmas*, especially those for boys, are adorned with bunches of feathers from colourful birds. *Cushmas* worn by men are always made from hand-woven materials. They are either white or rust brown and have dark vertical stripes. There is a split at the centre of the neckline at the front and back. Women's *cushmas* are made of smooth fabric and have broad horizontal necklines that enable them to nurse the infant hanging in the sling against their midriff.

Ashaninka fabrics are made with simple technology. The women work with a spindle weighted with a ceramic top. The top is turned in a dried half-gourd into which ash is scattered to reduce friction. Spun cotton is dyed in earthenware pots containing boiling water and natural pigments, such as bark or seedpods. Traditionally, reddish-brown and black are used for stripes in the fabric, but nowadays, synthetic yarn of other colours may also be used.

Ashaninka women carry their nursing infants against them almost the whole day long. The baby may sleep for a part of the day in an improvised hammock, but at night it sleeps with its mother. It is not unknown for children to be taken and eaten by a boa, a jaguar or an

Young woman with child in a tsompirontsi with decorated bones [A. Bant].

Below and right: Decorated bones from a tsompirontsi.

ocelot, and so parents are fearful of leaving a small child unattended, even for short periods on the veranda of the house.

The carrying strap, or *tsompirontsi*, is fashioned from hand-woven cotton. Small, flat, carved animal bones are attached to its underside. Both the production process of the carrier itself and the bones that hang from it have symbolic significance. They represent a 'test of competence' that young people must pass if they wish to establish their own family.

Women have lower social status than men in Amazonian tribal communities. However, the baby sling, insofar as it is a communal product of both sexes, can be seen as a symbolic expression of the importance the Ashaninka attach to the complementary nature of the 'female' and 'male' tasks in the family economy. The access of Ashaninka women to the important political processes of the family and community is limited, but their contribution to productivity is not undervalued. Women are greatly valued for their productive activities, especially in relation to agriculture.

Within these defined boundaries, women are able make autonomous decisions.

It still sometimes happens that when she first menstruates a girl must live for some time, up to a few months, in a small screened-off area in her parents' house. Female members of her family bring her food, and she spends her time spinning yarn. When the girl emerges, she is considered eligible for marriage. There is no comparable rite of passage for boys, but before a young couple can set up home, the boy must spend some time with his future father-in-law performing various tasks and services to prove that he can fulfil the male role in the household.

In anticipation of the marriage, the young woman makes the baby sling. In doing so, she proves that she possesses all the required agricultural skills: she cultivates the cotton, processes it, spins the yarn and weaves it. The man is expected to provide the entire family with fresh meat. He continually hunts, and for each animal that he kills, he presents his bride with a small carved bone, which is used to decorate the *tsompirontsi*. By the time the tsompirontsi has sufficient bones dangling from it, the first baby is usually already on its way. The couple can now begin to live their lives together.

Following the birth of the child, the *tsom pirontsi* takes on a second symbolic function. It protects the child from supernatural forces, the damaging influences of vengeful spirits and charms cast by jealous fellow villagers. Ashaninka believe that not only humans, but all animals and plants, and some objects too, possess souls. Both benign and malign spirits display human characteristics. Their behaviour is recognisable, and often predictable, to the Ashaninka. For example, the spirit of an animal killed in the hunt may seek revenge by causing the hunter or his blood relatives to become ill. In this belief system, the relationship with the environment is subject to manipulation. This process of manipulation – by appeasing, warding off influences and restoring damage – is an important component of religious and social activity.

Just how fearful traditional mothers can be of the harm that malign spirits might wreak on their children is illustrated by the fact that they do not simply dispose of its faeces. Excrement is wrapped in plant leaves, and these packages are kept in a knotted palm-leaf bag. When the bag is full, the contents are burned, buried or thrown in the river. In this way it is hoped that insects will not take possession of small particles of the faeces and use it to bewitch the child.

The small bones hanging from the sling are decorated with carved geometric figures that protect the child from the 'touch' of the malign spirits – in the normal course of events. The linear motifs and the clinking sound that the bones make as they knock against each other provide protection against evil, and hold sorcery at bay. The sound also serves as a warning to

Above and left: Decorated bones from a tsompirontsi.

the spirits, who appear in the form of light air currents.

The motifs on the bones are one of but a few decorations found on Ashaninkan implements. According to some anthropologists, the use of geometric motifs – rather than forms derived from nature – is inspired by the effects of hallucinatory plant extracts that adult men, and some adult women, drink in order to come into contact with the supernatural world. Before a trance state is reached, certain neural pathways are stimulated by chemicals in the drink. This causes a variety of visions of geometric shapes. The visions are associated with benign and protective spirits. The Ashaninka believe that regular use of this extract improves the human eye's ability to discern good spirits.

The reproduction of these visions as carvings on bones is an attempt to create and strengthen bonds with benign spirits. By wearing their symbols they hope to gain their favour.

Chapter 2.4.1

China

A thick lining brings prosperity and happiness

P. Bramlage

Children have been carried on the back for centuries in China. In bags, cloths, baskets, cots and slings. The means of transport for most of the one billion inhabitants of this vast country is either the bicycle or the bus, which is often full to overflowing. Prams are therefore impractical, although simple bamboo carts are used near home. Children therefore need to be conveyed by other means. The most obvious solution is for the child to be carried.

The simplest way to carry children is to strap them onto the back. Women do this when they cycle to work and drop their children off at the day nursery. The child stands on the bicycle's luggage rack bound to its mothers back. Positioned in this way, their feet cannot be caught between the spokes and they are protected from other road users. Most Chinese women have to work, but not all children can go to the day nursery, so children are often cared for by their grandparents. It is not unusual to see a child on its grandfather's back while he is shopping or on its grandmother's while she does the dishes. Housing is often cramped, and it is common for children, parents and grandparents all to live in one room. For this reason, many aspects of domestic life take place outdoors: cooking, eating and doing homework for example. Boys tend to be valued more highly than girls despite campaigns to redress the balance. In general, boys receive preferential treatment. They are also carried for longer, sometimes even up to the age of five.

In the large cities, parents or grandparents often use simple slings of sheets with straps to carry their young. This is not the case in the countryside.

In Xinjiang, in the far northwest of China, live the Uygurs, an Islamic people who speak a language more closely resembling Turkish than Chinese. They also write using an Arabic script. They have partially preserved their traditional costume and rituals. Some Uygurs live in Turfan, which is 155 metres below sea level; it is the hottest region in China during the summer. With summer temperatures as high as 47°C, and winters well below freezing point, the Uygurs live in an extreme climate.

The town of Turfan has only a few streets, a market and some dusty dirt tracks. Travelling is done on foot or by donkey cart. Houses are built of clay, mud and straw. There are few household goods except for finely crafted chests and coloured earthenware. The people work small fields of cotton and other produce. They use carry-cots to transport their children. These cots are preferable to slings in such a harsh climate; during the summer it is too hot to carry a child against one's body. The cots can be carried over the shoulder or by donkey cart.

In the summer, out on the fields, children are placed safely under a lean-to to protect them from heat and insects. In the cold of winter, they lie snugly in the cot, wrapped under their colourful blankets. They are removed from the cot like a package, tied as they are to the mattress. The baby is barely able to move when in the cot because embroidered straps bind its arms and legs. Indoors, the cots are often hung raised from the floor and can swing. The cots, straps and clothes are cheerfully coloured. Red, the colour of happiness, is often used – not only here but throughout China. Stylised floral and geometric motifs, common in Islamic cultures, are used by the Uygurs in their embroidery and carving. The cots are also finely carved.

The little-known Xishuangbanna is the southernmost prefecture of Yunnan Province in southwest China. Many different minorities live here. Each have their own language, religion and customs, as well as their own traditional costume, usually beautifully woven or embroidered. One of the larger minorities is the Dai with a population of around 850,000. Dai means 'freedom' – an ironic name for a minority population in China. They are Buddhists. They have lived in Xishuangbanna's humid tropical climate since the thirteenth century. They live in houses built on poles; pigs and chickens scratch around underneath them. Women wear sarongs and large straw hats. They carry their children in the sarongs, usually on the hip. On their backs they carry loads of wood or crops from the fields. The children are carried in this way to the fields. Enormous distances are covered on foot along the narrow jungle paths; there are few passable roads but there is also a certain amount of simple river traffic.

This baby carrier has been appliquéd with multicoloured pieces of cloth, creating geometric figures.
[All photographs in the chapter China by P. Bramlage]

This Sani woman in Shiliu has a baby carrier of firmly quilted green velvet. The central square is embroidered with cross-stitch, with plenty of red – the colour of happiness.

In another region in the south of the Yunnan, Han Chinese women use a baby carrier that is a cross between a sling and a bag. The child is carried in a square sheet of robust fabric. This sheet is lined, and reinforced with layers of quilted material between the lining and the embroidered outer layer. The flowers are embroidered onto black velvet using satin stitch. A strap is sewn at each corner, and these are used to secure the carrier by tying. The child is, as it were, clamped between the mother's back and the stiffly lined bag. Small babies' legs stay inside the bag, while older children's dangle out of it.

In China, the symbolism of objects lies in their decoration. Babies' bonnets, collars and shoes may be decorated in a rich variety of ways: tiger shapes, for example, that offer protection against danger and malign spirits, or coins that promise prosperity. Decorations frequently feature five leaves or wings. Traditionally, the number five is associated with the five blessings: a long life, good health, wealth or high social status, love and a natural death. In modern-day China, the number five represents the 'five guarantees': housing, food, clothing, medical care and funeral costs. The number five also appears as part of a rural custom, especially among mountain tribes: the fifth day of the fifth month is considered to

Two images of Sao Bin in Yunnan province. In the upper photograph a Bai couple is seen walking to the market in Sao Bin. The man carries the child on his back and the woman carries the basket containing wares.

be a dangerous day in a child's life. To protect it from harm, the child then receives an apron embroidered using a special technique. It is colourfully decorated with poisonous creatures such as snakes, scorpions and insects, along with tigers and other guardian animals.

It was customary in former times for the grandmother to make both the carrier and the apron. She ensured that everything was complete by the end of the baby's first month. Nowadays, many women receive a carrier, decorated with the various symbols, as a wedding gift. The colours also have symbolic meanings, but it is no longer always possible to identify them. Red, in any case, is common to all communities and represents happiness. White usually represents death or mourning. Should one of the parents die, the carrier is turned inside out and the embroidered side is hidden from view. According to custom a woman can create a new design, and in this way embroidery and weaving traditions are kept alive.

With a population of around five million, the

Yi is one of the largest minorities in southern China. Yi is the collective name for several dozen population groups. One of these groups is the Sani, who are renowned for their cross-stitch embroidery applied to delicate fabrics. Sani women generally wear magnificent traditional attire. The embroidery closely resembles that of the Yao in Thailand, and they use similar motifs and colours. In the past, motifs had symbolic meanings as well as decorative value, but because women develop traditional patterns freely – using new materials, techniques and colours – their symbolic significance has been degraded. It is therefore sometimes extremely difficult to discern any resemblance between modern and traditional designs. On a baby carrier, a serpentine geometric pattern symbolises long life, and star-shaped motifs stand for happiness and wealth. The colour red, representing happiness, is often used on carriers.

The Dali area of Yunnan province is an ancient and fascinating region, known since the pre-Christian era. In the eighth century AD the city of Tali (present-day Dali) was capital of the Nanzhao Empire; it is now a city with a population of 3 million. It has a remarkable architecture, and even today buildings may only be built in the traditional style. Dali and the surrounding region is inhabited by the Bai, a population group of around one million who are spread over several provinces and are known by a variety of names. They maintain their traditional music, dance and clothing. In addition to their many weaving and embroidery techniques they use the *plangi* technique, which is a method of dying that involves tying off different parts of the fabric. Some of the traditional Bai costume is made using this technique. It is usually worn by older women, but in some villages young girls also wear it. Designs vary according to village and age group. Embroidered clothing worn by young girls living around Dali and Sao Bin, a small market town, are notable for their exuberant use of colour. A variety of techniques are used in the creation of an article of clothing, and it is completed by the application of shiny embroidered bands bought at the market. These are decorated with many colours – including an abundance of gold thread. The Bai are very fond of flowers, and 'Golden Flower' is a much-loved girl's name. In their handiwork, they often use stylised lotus blossoms as well as birds and butterflies.

Although nowadays embroidered fabrics intended for use on clothing and baby carriers are available at markets, most girls still embroider their own clothing, and most carriers are made by the baby's grandmother. Girls learn their craft from a very early age. The Bai claim they can gain an insight into the character of the craftswoman by studying her creations: they can tell if the maker is lazy or industrious, slapdash or conscientious, dull or original – and whether she is diligent and therefore a suitable wife.

In the past, baby carriers had extremely thick linings consisting of five layers, representing the five blessings. Nowadays, they may be made with a single thick layer, representing happiness. The underside of many carriers is made with an unusual appliqué technique that creates an effect somewhat resembling stained glass, and is known as the 'cathedral window'. The frayed corners of the windows are sometimes finished off with small metal balls, or alternatively they may be completed with pieces of fabric. The embroidery occasionally features a decorative white shape: a ram's horn or a bat, for example. The bat symbolises happiness and wealth.

Bats, butterflies and ducks are some of the many symbols for happiness in China; pomegranates symbolise fertility, and lotus blossoms, a long and happy life, reliability and purity. An oblique lozenge stands for victory. Leaves and leaf motifs ensure good health. Waves or connected triangles describe the borderline between life and death. Fish signify fidelity in marriage and loyalty in general. The infinite knot is thought to bring about both fertility and happiness in marriage. Stars simply bring happiness, and serpents symbolise long life. A diagonal cross protects the bearer from misfortune and extends his life.

Chapter 2.4.2

Java
Symbol of femininity

R. Heringa

The Javanese baby sling is closely associated with women. It is an indispensable aid worn while performing many activities, and it appears in many forms. The Javanese costume is carefully composed; form and function are closely linked. A woman's clothing is quite simple – it consists only of two long pieces of cloth of varying widths – but with it she can express a broad range of symbolic messages. Choice of fabric, size, decorative techniques, colour combinations and motifs can all contribute to the message. Most important is the relationship between the various elements. Although there have been regular developments throughout history, it appears that recent additions are often rooted in ancient traditional systems of meaning.

The two pieces of fabric vary between two and three metres in length, and from half a metre to more than a metre in width. The broad version is a *tapih wijar*, but is often referred to using the Indonesian term *kain panjang*. Mainly used as a hip cloth, it is worn by both men and women. It is less well known that the cloth can also serve as a baby sling. The narrower *tapih ciyut* is exclusively female attire. The size and type of fabric selected is determined by its intended function, but equally it can indicate the social rank of the wearer. Until the beginning of the twentieth century, woven or batik fabrics were chosen especially for this purpose. Nowadays, the fashion is for material printed with batik motifs, or even plain cloth, bought by the metre. Symbolism has declined in importance.

The narrow cloth can be worn in a multitude of ways and has many names. A market woman may wear an expansive and sturdy cotton cloth over her shoulders to lug around her wares, while a sophisticated woman in the city might wear a fine transparent plain fabric over her shoulder as an elegant element of her attire for an official reception. Throughout much of Indonesia, this kind of shoulder cloth is called a *slendang*.

The most widespread function of the cloth is directly related to what is seen as the woman's most important task: motherhood. Babies and toddlers find a safe haven in the sling. Here too, there are variations in style. The narrower cloth is not used as a baby sling at the central Javanese royal courts or in aristocratic Javanese families. Instead, a broad hip cloth is used, which is batiked with central Javanese motifs in subdued red-browns and blue-blacks. The relatively large cloth indicates something of the baby's high social ranking. However, less affluent central Javanese use fabrics of a similar size and style, although they will be decorated using a cheaper batik stamp method or be factory printed.

Along the northern coast and in the larger cities a large brightly coloured batik cloth called a *gendhongan* is found, which is almost

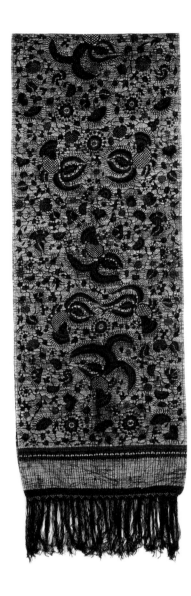

generally not the mother who carried the baby. Social status was again expressed by the size of the baby sling. Nowadays, the machine-printed *gendhongan* is a cheap mass-produced product that can be purchased almost anywhere, and it has become conventional attire for the urbanite.

Traditional handiwork has fallen into disuse. Only in a few villages, in the region surrounding the centuries-old East Javanese harbour village of Tuban, does the craft survive, due to the tenacious efforts of the women. They make the broad and narrow batik fabrics in traditional style for use in their own communities. In recent years, however, they have produced modern designs for trade outside the region.

The meaning of the word *sayut*, the local term for the baby sling, is closely associated with femininity. It can mean 'wrapping around' or 'encircling', or 'united, mutually supportive'. In old Javanese, *sayut* also meant 'a means of protection against misfortune or disease'. The actual making of the cloth is performed by the three generations of women who live together on one estate. The importance of this activity is apparent from the special role of the demonic female ancestor who is known under a number of mysterious names such as *Nyi Diwut*, (shaggy-haired grandmother) or *Nyi Towong* (invisible grandmother): she can only been discerned at full moon as a ghostly shadow sitting at her spinning wheel. While women are at work they are all too aware of the all-seeing eye of their much-feared instructress watching over them.

The colours that the dyer applies to the batiked fabric are laden with significance. The depth and combination of colours indicate to which age group and village the wearer belongs. To make herself recognisable to others, a woman will wrap the cloth around her as soon as she leaves her own land. At the regional marketplace, women from different villages are easily recognised by the gradations of colour. Furthermore, the choice of

Pipitan, the elaborate three-coloured gift from the maternal grandmother. Large black and white quails flutter through a tangle of flowering vines.
[The slings shown in this chapter are the property of the author.]

equal in size to the broad hip cloth. It is divided up in a different way, however: the stripes perpendicular to the short sides indicate that it is a shoulder cloth (page 96). The *gendhongan* (*gendhong* means 'to carry') is specially made as a baby sling. This type of cloth was originally used by families of mixed Chinese-Indonesian or European-Indonesian ancestry. Evidence of these origins can be found in the 'European' and 'Chinese' motifs: irises, chrysanthemums, peonies and mythical birds and animals. Among these often well-to-do citizens, it was

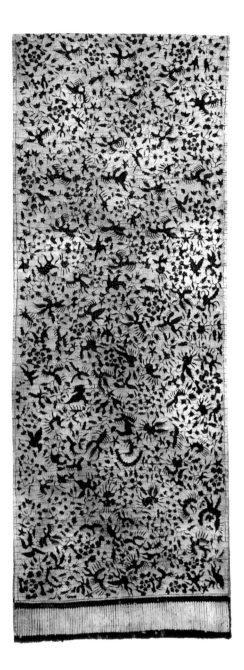

Putihan, the protective blue and white gift from the paternal grandmother. The intricate motif on this antique cloth is called manuk miber, birds that fly out when danger approaches. The fringe was probably cut off during a ritual.

The *sayut* functions as a replacement womb. From the first moment of life (which according to Javanese tradition begins three months before birth) until seven months after birth, the immediate social circle focuses on providing for the welfare of mother and child. It is a period of socialisation during which adaptation and the adoption of the new member of the community is facilitated by a series of rituals. Three groups of relatives contribute: those from the mother's side, those from the father's side and finally a group of (mythical) ancestral figures that represent the totality of cosmic forces. Various baby slings play a role: they express a variety of symbolic meanings depending on the event.

In addition to social rank, the baby sling can convey something of the relationship between two people or groups. The relationship between the grandmothers on the one hand and the young mother and child on the other is integrated in the complexity of the baby slings that the grandmothers present to the new mother. The grandmother on the mother's side makes the most elaborate cloth with no more than three colours. The vivid red and indigo blue motifs stand out against the softly marbled blue background. There are black accents where the colours have mixed during painting. This blending expresses the close bond between man and woman, grandparents, parents and children or grandchildren within the community. With this gift, the baby is acknowledged as the third link in the series of generations. The name given to the sling, *pipitan*, meaning 'closely joined together' further confirms this connection.

The paternal grandmother contributes a sling of a single colour: vivid blue motifs contrast with a plain background. In order to achieve the most powerful visual effect, it is of great importance that the wax used is of high quality and that the drawings are executed with great care. This sling is known as *putihan*, 'pure' or 'purifying'. The concept of purifica-

colours, the way the cloth is folded, and the accompanying ornaments indicate whether the wearer is on her way to market, to a wedding or to bring food to her husband working in the fields.

Just like its name, *sayut*, the form and function of the baby sling reflect feminine qualities. The message contained in the form is communicated by way the cloth is divided, the motifs and colour combinations. As a result, the cloth becomes, as it were, the personification of the carrier.

tion refers to the protective function attributed to the blue and white baby sling; it will be brought into service whenever the child suffers illness or misfortune for many years to come. Over time, the sling accumulates power – as long as the rule proscribing washing is obeyed. According to the Javanese system of colour classification, blue and white belong to the northeast. In the infinitely repeating life cycle, this is the otherworldly region between death (north) and new life (east).

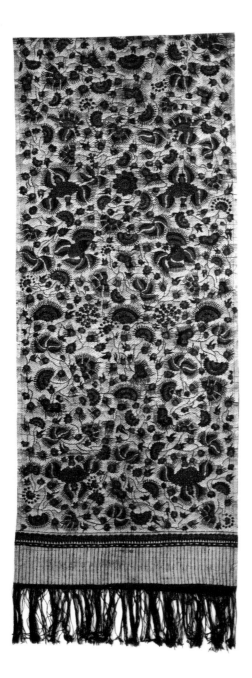

Especially at times of potential danger, such as the birth of the child, there is a need for an extra force external to the immediate community. The grandparents on the father's side are 'others', and they can provide this power. This is perhaps more accurately illustrated by a second meaning of the word *putihan*. It is used to describe people who refrained from 'earthly' contacts. In practice, the relationship between the baby and the grandmother on the father's side is distant. Not only does the grandmother belong to a distant community that may be located several hours walk away, but by presenting the sling she defines herself as belonging to an outer, or even supernatural, region.

Thus, the colours and terms used for the two slings clearly characterise the hierarchical relationship between the grandmother belonging to the group and the grandmother related only by marriage. This division is also demonstrated by the way the sling is used. The *pipitan* is for general daily use, while the *putihan* only appears for ritualistic purposes – when the child is ill or cries a lot, for example. The blue-and-white sling is thought to facilitate healing. The fringed end of the cloth is considered especially powerful. It is draped over the child's head or used to dry its tears. Its effect can be magnified by dipping a corner in flower-scented water.

The third 'grandmother' is the *dukun bayi*, the midwife. She functions as a conduit between the community and supernatural forces. Her magical and life-giving knowledge is passed on from generation to generation. Her mother's and her grandmother's graves are sanctuaries for villagers in difficulty. *Nyi Dukun* (Grandmother Midwife) prepares fortifying and medicinal herbal drinks and massages the future mother to ensure a successful birth. She also shows family members how to perform complex rituals. During delivery she demonstrates how the father must support his wife's back. Following the birth, the placenta is wrapped in a piece of undyed cotton and

Putihan, the red and white cloth in which the father carries the placenta, the 'younger brother', to the back door. The birds and flowers have healing and life-giving properties.

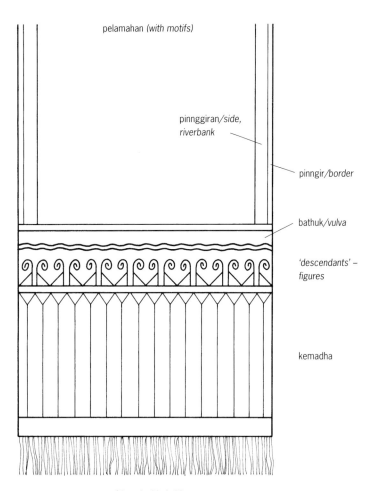

pelamahan (with motifs)

pinnggiran/side, riverbank

pinngir/border

bathuk/vulva

'descendants' – figures

kemadha

fringe/'pubic hair'

Gendhongan. *The gendhongan consists of a central area called the pelemahan (land for cultivation or building) surrounded by a series of borders, which are long and narrow along the selvedge and wider with long fringes on the short sides. The wide border features stylised motifs that have been described as geometric – batik publications have never been clear about their significance. The name of the vertical stripes, pengadha or kemadha, has been translated as 'needle edge' and explained as an imitation fringe. However, village women provided a more direct and expressive explanation. And if we look at the composition as a whole, the symbolism becomes immediately apparent. The key to the mystery is the term bathuk used for one of the border patterns. It means 'vulva' and shows that the sayut is seen as the body of a woman. The hemmed area is the womb and the entrance to it is the vulva. Giggling shyly, the women explain that the long fringes represent pubic hair. The border of stylised 'human' figures, which consist mainly of two legs, possibly represent the progeny. The motifs in the central area – birds and flowers, living creatures of heaven and earth – established the bearer's creative role in the universe. The abundance plant life relates to the water that brings fertility.*

placed in an earthenware pot. The young father carries this in a red and white *sayut* to the back door, and buries it there.

The navel is considered the central point of the body and the entrance through which life is passed from mother to child. An oil lamp is set on the tiny burial mound next to the door, and burns day and night until the baby's

umbilical cord falls off. From this moment, the direct connection between mother and child ceases to exist. This transition too is overseen by the midwife. As darkness falls at the end of the afternoon, she comes to the new parents' home for the last time to wash the baby and swaddle it in soft pieces of cloth made from household members' well-worn clothes. For the first time the child will be dressed in sewn, 'proper' clothing: a rectangular piece of flannel wrapped sarong-style around the lower body and a Dutch woolly hat with a pompom to protect the fontanelle. These gifts from the father's family are purchased at the market along with the colourful machine-printed *gendhongan* and a new set of clothes for the mother. Even more than with the *putihan*, the father's family clearly gain prestige with the bestowal of this last gift, associated as it is with the city and the outside world, which has higher status.

During the evening, close family members and neighbours gather at the baby's home. The baby's name, symbol of its individual identity within the community, is made known. The midwife takes the splendidly dressed child and introduces it to the female guests. She uses her three-coloured *pipitan*, woven from natural reddish-brown cotton. As the personification of the invisible ancestor, she is the only person permitted to carry this sling. In turn, each of the other women take the child in their arms and place it in their own sling. The child is not put down for the duration of the event. It remains within the group to signify its acceptance by the community.

In early life, the baby sling functions largely as accommodation and sanctuary. Initially the baby lies in it almost naked. Carrying her baby on the left hip and supporting it with one arm, the mother can react to the slightest sign of its need to drink. The flap hanging from the sling is used to fan the child or protect its head in the full heat of the day. If the mother needs to use both hands, the baby is shifted to her back. Thus positioned, upright in the sling with its head against her neck, it can sleep on.

In its seventh month, the baby's feet are set on the ground for the first time. The method of carrying changes during this period: the child's awareness of the surroundings increases and when awake it sits upright in the sling. Initially the legs stretch forward, but as the baby grows, its legs dangle from the sling and straddle the mother's hips – one in front and one behind.

Only after the baby has taken its first steps does its sling fall gradually into disuse. For a long time yet however, it will serve as a refuge during afternoon naps and at mealtimes. When the child is about three years old, there is often a younger brother or sister making a claim on the sling. The process of socialisation is complete, and the *sayut* has played a central role in the process

The naturally reddish-brown fabric forms the basis for the midwife's baby sling. The motif is called kembang kluwek. *It depicts the flowers of the tree from which the midwife obtains the intoxicating seeds she uses as a medicine.*

Chapter 2.4.3

Borneo

Tiger teeth for aristocratic babies

Herbert L. Whittier
Patricia R. Whittier

At first glance, the baby carrier, or *ba'*, used by the Kenyah Dayak of central Borneo appears to be simply a utilitarian, if highly ornate, object that is functionally comparable with the baby-carriers now used in the west, or the slings used all over the world. However, the *ba'* is not only a useful item, it is often a work of art, and also has a spiritual and social role in the life of the Kenyah.

The Kenyah *ba'* is usually constructed of finely woven rattan, with a heavier rattan frame and a crescent-shaped seat. Woven rattan straps are attached to allow the adult or older child to carry the baby on his or her back; the baby normally faces the adult's back with its legs straddling the adult at about waist level. From this position the baby can observe the passing scene or sleep with its head resting on the adult's shoulder or back. The *ba'* is used from birth until the child is two years old or more. For a long trip, such as that between village and fields, even a four-year-old may be carried in a *ba'*. When the infant is very tiny, the *ba'* is padded with a thin pillow and may have a padded booster seat in it. It may also be carried in front rather than on the back, a more convenient position for nursing. If it is carried on the back, the adult ties a sarong or other cloth around the *ba'* and around the child's own waist to better secure the carrier.

The complete carrier has several parts. First is the *ba'* itself – the wood and rattan structure. The standards of the craftsmen are applied here: is the wood seat carefully smoothed?

Simple Kenyah carry basket. Only the edges are decorated with fabric. Additional embellishments are snail shells for the dried umbilical cord, a taro shoot and small pieces of taro root. These ritual objects are important during the chut tanah ceremony, when the child touches the earth for the first time and receives its name. Lang Moh, Baram River, Sarawak, Malaysia, 1975.

[All photographs in this chapter by H.L and P.R Whittier]

Is the frame strong and securely attached to the seat? Is the rattan back finely woven, with the ends of the rattan turned back? Are the straps properly fastened with good pineapple-fibre cord?

The second component of the *ba'* is the lining and edging. The edges are covered with a patchwork strip made of colourful pieces of cloth. For some children, particularly those of the lowest social ranks, this is the extent of the *ba'*, but for most there is a great deal more. The *ba'* customarily has beading covering the back. This beadwork piece, or *aban*, is made of tiny seed beads woven into a design of about 25 by 35cm that is sewn onto the *ba'*. The designs that may be used are fairly standardised, as are the colours, although this may be subject to the availability of beads. The preferred main colours are black, yellow and white, with touches of red, green, blue and others for highlights.

The beading of the *aban* is the most time-consuming aspect of ba' construction. A woman working in her spare time can make one in about three months, depending on the season. The designs have many curlicues and flowing curves, and a good bead-worker is one who can make these curves smooth, narrowing down to one bead in width. Around the edge of the *aban* may be round decorations such as pieces of shell, buttons or, especially on the Indonesian side of the border, old Dutch silver coins.

The kinds of designs used on the *ba'* can be grouped into three broad categories. The first type is one with a full human figure as its central motif. The figure is very stylised, portrayed in a seated position, and executed in typical Kenyah style with curvilinear designs emanating from the head, hands, and feet. Only those of the highest social ranking, the *deta'u*, may use this design – whether on a *ba'* or on other objects. The second type of design employs only a human head; again executed in stylised form with curved lines emanating

from it. This design may be used by lesser aristocrats, or *deta'u dumit*. A third design consisting of abstract curved forms may be used by commoners. Other motifs may occasionally be used in the beadwork along with the central design. Again, these motifs are restricted by social rank. The tiger, for example, would only be used by a *deta'u* person.

The final aspect of *ba'* decoration is the attachment of objects that hang by short strings from the back and sides of the carrier. Some are essential, some are dictated by the infant's sex and class, and others are individual. Every *ba'* has at least one shell of a large snail, and preferably two – for the noise they make clacking together. When the infant's umbilical cord falls off, it is placed in one of these shells. Animal teeth are an addition mediated by the infant's sex and class. Tiger teeth can be used only for aristocratic infants, the number varying with the degree of social status and sex. It should be noted that tigers are not indigenous to Borneo, and tiger teeth are extremely valuable goods owned only by *deta'u* families. Panther teeth are also used by the *deta'u*. Old heirloom beads may be attached to the *ba'* too. Some old beads are considered so valuable that in the days before European rule, they could be used to purchase a human being (war captives). Many of these beads have individual names of their own and are venerated by all.

Last, the type of design on the *aban* and the associated objects hung on the *ba'* together signal social ranking. The symbols used by the high-ranking people are considered to be the most powerful. For a lower ranking person to use them would be to invite illness or even death. It is interesting to note that although the symbols of social ranking are disappearing in other contexts especially among the Christian Kenyah, they continued to appear on the *ba'* and on coffins. Perhaps this is because the souls of both infants and the newly deceased are in dangerous transition. The danger is not only to the individual and his or her soul, but

Elaborately decorated ba's, each with at least six tiger teeth and many leopard teeth. The edges are decorated with old Dutch coins. A stylised human figure is depicted on each beadwork aban. Ba's such as these are intended for children from the highest social rank, the deta'u. Lepo Tau Kenyah, Kalimantan Timur, Indonesia, 1970.

also to families and neighbours should evil forces tamper with a soul in transition.

Other groups living in central Borneo use the *ba'*, including the Kayan, Sebop, Kanowit, Berawan, Punan and Kajang. Only the Kenyah, however, seem to have elaborated its decoration into a demonstration of social ranking. While the other groups use similar designs, they do not necessarily associate particular designs with social classes. This is, of course, not only true of the use of these designs on the *aban ba'*, but also of their more general use.

The first major event in the new infant's life is called the *petakau anak* (literally 'free the child') or *chut tana* ('to touch the earth'). This ceremony serves several purposes for both the mother and the infant. It takes place two to four weeks after the birth, the exact day depending on the appropriate phase of the moon.

The *petakau anak* ceremony frees the mother from the postpartum prohibitions on certain foods, on bathing, and on leaving the house. The baby receives its name and is formally introduced and brought into the Kenyah community. Spirits that might do the baby harm are enjoined to stay away, while good spirits are encouraged to hover nearby. This event is also the first time that the baby leaves the house, and it does so in a *ba'*. For this first journey the *ba'* is decorated only with the snail shells containing the dried stump of the umbilical cord and pieces of certain plants gathered earlier that day from the forests. The baby, in the *ba'* on the mother's back, is carried down from the house to the ground in a small procession with its father, one of two of the elderly women who are usually in charge of such ceremonies, and a young sibling (or cousin) of the opposite sex. On the ground, the child is introduced to some of the implements and activities of its later life. If the child is a boy, there is a mock hunt in which the adults place his hand on a spear to 'kill' a pig made of a banana with twig legs. A baby girl uses a net to 'catch' a dried fish. After the group return to the house, everyone gets a tiny bite of the pig or fish and praises the child's skill in feeding the family. There are several other parts to this ceremony, but this is the only one in which the *ba'* plays a major role (P. Whittier, 1981: 61-62).

The *ba'* itself and the act of being carried in it become sources of security for very young children. A frightened or tired toddler often climbs onto an adult's back saying *"ba' me"*, or 'carry me'. Adults encourage such behaviour: we have often heard adults, in situations they perceived to be frightening or threatening, call to a child *"ba', ba'"* either to remove the child from danger or just to be a closer. In either case, the small child develops a sense that the *ba'* and the adult's back are safe havens. The *ba'* is not only a place of safety, it is also a source of comfort. The major method of soothing a tired or cranky infant or young child is to walk with it in the *ba'* up and down the veranda of the long house, usually with a rhythmic gait punctuated with snatches of a song or chant. A mother who is trying to prepare a meal with a crying infant or whining

toddler on her hands will order an older child *" ba' sadinko"*, or 'carry your younger sibling'. The protection afforded by the *ba'* goes beyond that of simply being close to an adult. The Kenyah, like many people throughout the world, traditionally believed that infants' souls were not very well attached to their bodies and that the failure of the soul to stay close was a cause of illness and perhaps death. Even among those now professing Christianity, this belief persists. The *ba'* works in two ways to keep the infant healthy. First, its decoration is attractive to the infant soul, and the soul will stay nearby. The second, the various objects hung on the *ba'* and the noises they make will repel evil spirits that might want to entice the soul away. We often observed the inexperienced young mothers being encouraged by their mothers and other older women to carry their small babies in the *ba'* almost constantly, particularly if the infant seemed weak or sickly. If the sick baby is not actually being carried in the *ba'*, the *ba'* will be close by. Thus, the *ba'* is the child's refuge from both visible and invisible hazards.

In addition to being a practical item for carrying a baby, a social guardian of the baby's health and a display of status, the *ba'* is also regarded as a beautiful object, a work of art. Like most fieldworkers, we were often asked to make family portrait photographs for which the family would dress in their finest clothes and pose very formally. The family usually arranged to have the smallest child's *ba'* included in the picture, either by having the mother turned to make the carrier at least partially visible or by simply placing it on the ground in the front of the group.

The social relations engendered are strengthened by the assembly and construction of the *ba'* are one of its more interesting aspects. The construction of the basic wooden seat with the woven rattan back and straps is generally a household enterprise. Women usually do the fine rattan work and men the carving of the seat and the attaching of the woven part to the seat with a heavier rattan frame. These are skills well within the range of any adults of the appropriate sex. Thus, the work may be done by the child's parents, grandparents, aunts or uncles. Alternatively, the *ba'* may be one previously used by a sibling or cousin. In this case, if the sibling or cousin is old enough to have given up the *ba'*, the decoration will have been removed, and the *ba'* will be redecorated for the new baby. The initial *ba'* decorations, the snail shells and pieces of root used for the *petakau* ceremony, are usually gathered by elderly women, the grandmothers or great-aunts of the baby. It is for the later, more elaborate, decorations that the network must extend beyond the household. The first items to be obtained are the small 'seed' beads for the *aban*. Since the beading is a lengthy task, it begins before the birth of the child. In areas near bazaars, beads may be simply purchased for relatively small sums. In more remote areas, however, the accumulation of sufficient beads is more problematic and their trade value rises enormously. Traders from other areas, being without kin ties in the village, feel free to demand in goods whatever the market will bear – often equivalent to twenty times or more the price of the beads in the bazaar. Women in the village may also trade among themselves, often exchanging beads in an attempt to gather the appropriate mix of colours. Some colours are in higher demand than others, so this trade often takes the form of 'I'll trade you one-and-a-half strings of red for one of black'. Within the village, one is restrained, of course, from driving the kinds of bargains that outside traders can. After the beads are obtained, the decoration of the *aban* begins. This work is usually done by older women, partly because they are more skilled in beadwork and partly because they are freer of the daily demands of domestic and agricultural work. Commonly it is a grandmother of

the expected child who does the beading. In recent years, a few people have begun to bead *aban* for outright sale, but this is still rare.

To obtain the other decorative elements for the *ba'* one must have recourse not to traders but to kinsmen. The coins, animal teeth, large beads, and other items used, are heirloom goods that are not available for sale but must be borrowed from their current custodians. It should be noted that these items have uses other than the *ba'* decoration and may therefore be in demand for other purposes. We have stated that a certain items and the numbers of these items that may be used are associated with degrees of social rank. Only a *deta'u* person, for example, can possess tiger teeth. Therefore, one must have recourse to other *deta'u* to obtain the tiger teeth necessary for the *ba'* of a baby of *deta'u* rank. Likewise, fine heirloom beads are owned only by *deta'u*. To have such beads displayed on the *ba'* is an indication of the baby's rank and also the validation of that rank by other *deta'u* in that they have loaned the beads for that purpose.

Thus, the *ba'* not only visually displays the status of its occupant, it also organises a group of kinsmen around a new member of the group. People will point out their individual contributions to a *ba'*. By saying 'I gave this bead and those two tiger teeth' a person is saying indirectly 'I am a person of high social rank'. A Kenyah would never say this directly, presumption being dangerous behaviour, but he wants the fact to be known. Through their use of the *ba'*, items of heirloom wealth are recombined and redistributed for each new member of the group, confirming the child as a group member and revalidating the positions of those who contribute the goods and their ties to their ancestors. One unusual aspect of the ties of reciprocity that are generated by the *ba'* is that, unlike their ties established and confirmed by such activities as the distribution of wild animal meat after a hunt, a joint travel venture, or a joint labour on a

Petakau anak ceremony. Mother and child walk on the ground for the first time since the birth. The ba' is decorated with snail shells, roots and leaves with a ritual significance. Lepo, Tau Kenyah, Sarawak, Malaysia, 1974.

new house, these ties are among women. The mother and grandmothers of the child will most likely approach other women to obtain the goods. They may ultimately come from men (for example, a woman may request a pair of tiger teeth from a female cousin who may actually get them from her own father), but they pass through women and thus reinforce and establish relationships among women.

The ties between pairs of men and women, and especially between *deta'u* individuals, lessen a tendency towards village schism. In modern Kenyah society, there are many forces that might encourage division and migration, including religious differences and the desire to be nearer to markets, schools, and health care. It is the social relationships established among the *deta'u* that moderate these forces. The use of heirloom goods on the *ba'* does more than simply identify *deta'u* by the use of symbols; it draws them into interaction and reinforces a consciousness of kin ties and common heritage. Even for those men who entertain ideas about schism and migration, the ties among their mothers, wives and daughters may be powerful countervailing forces.

Thus, what might appear to be a utilitarian item of material culture, a seat for carrying an infant, has multiple ramifications in Kenyah society. The *ba'* is a baby carrier, a work of art, a device for protecting a child's health, a display and confirmation of social rank, and a mechanism for creating and strengthening social relations.

Chapter 2.4.4

Central Asia

The healing properties of a willow cradle

T. Emelianenko

The rituals surrounding the birth and nurturing of children in Central Asia are centuries old. Most predate Islam, and others were introduced with Islam.[1] Many traditional elements of ceremonies dedicated to children, which ensure prosperity and good health, are still practised in rural areas. However, they have often lost much of their original meaning. They are now performed purely symbolically and out of custom.

The Tajik, Uzbek, Turkmen, Kirghiz and Kazak and other peoples of Central Asia considered a large number of children to be a sign of prosperity and the perpetuation of the bloodline. Reproduction is the sacred duty of all honourable people. As a local saying goes: 'the lives of fish depend on water, the lives of humans depend on children'. Work to ensure the baby's health and prosperity begins before birth, and concerns for its welfare are expressed by practical actions and a range of magical rituals. For these reasons, great importance is attached to the making and acquisition of the cradle, the first time the child is laid in the cradle, and a period in the cradle that is comfortable and free of danger.

Traditional cradles in Central Asia can be divided into two types: those made of wood, and those made in the form of a hammock from a piece of felt or napless double fabric. Wooden cradles are made of willow. The willow is considered to be one of the 'purest' and 'lightest' of trees. In the past, the sedentary populations of Central Asia attributed sacred qualities to the willow. People would sit under a willow tree for its healing effects. Many agricultural implements are made of willow. Even biers, intended to ease the deceased's passage into heaven by mitigating his sins, are made of it. The cradle of 'pure' willow protects the baby from malign spirits and ensures light and good sleep. In springtime in Baisun, southern Uzbekistan, a young willow branch is attached to the cradle, or small leaves are glued to it.

Craftsmen build up their own supply of willow. They seek the trees far from the village, because chopping trees within it is considered sinful. The wood may only be worked after having dried for one year. Workshops of the artisans who make cradles can be found in cities and large *kishlaks* (Central Asian villages). The cradle may also be made at home if the family has no money or no opportunity to buy one.

Cradles can be divided into three types according to outward appearance: the unpainted

---

[1] It is noteworthy that in birth, marriage and burial ceremonies, which are associated with the most important phases of human life, it is especially those elements that predate Islam that predominate among the Islamic peoples of Central Asian.

cradle, the cradle painted with colours, and the cradle with engraved ornamentation. Unpainted cradles used to be the most common, and in Samarkand, old artisans still consider this to be the purest variety. They are of the opinion that the magical power of the wood is of such magnitude that its surface forms a unified whole with the 'purity' of the spirit. Therefore, no extra decorations or symbols are necessary.

Other cradles are painted with geometric patterns and depictions of plants. Floral ornamentation includes flowers, leaves and climbing plants. These symbolise a long and flourishing life. Colours are generally vivid, and red – the colour of love, well-being and social status – predominates. The use of contrasting colours is intended to draw benign spirits to the child and ward off malign spirits, so the child will have a joyful and contented life. The geometric patterns are older and have an ancient sacred meaning for the local population. Tajiks living in the mountains and headland of the Pamira region, who are direct descendants of the original inhabitants of Central Asia, decorate their cradles in this way.

A geometric pattern consists of a combination of lozenges, squares, triangles, polygons and circles. Their meanings correspond largely with those of patterns used by other peoples elsewhere in the world. They relate the way the universe is said to have come into existence, the place of humans within it, and their harmonious relationship with nature. The cross – whether oblique or straight, on its own or accompanied by other figures – was extremely popular in Central Asian ornamentation. According to the local population, it is a diagrammatic representation of the human figure and depicts a spirit that wards off evil, especially the evil eye.[2]

The furnishing of the wooden cradle is of course a practical matter, but there are sacral overtones. A cotton mattress is laid in the bottom of the cradle. This is filled with straw and millet husks – not only for its softness and absorbency, but also because of its magical function: to protect and ensure good fortune.[3] In the mattress and the sheet, and the bottom of the cradle itself, there are holes. The child lies on its back, a flat pillow under its head. The baby's urine passes out of the cradle into a chamber pot through a wooden or bone tube, specially designed either for a boy or a girl. The child is covered with a blanket and then fastened into the cradle with broad straps. One of these crosses over the chest and is pulled down to the underside of the bed, thus pressing

This is a wooden cradle from Tajikistan, a tavora. *In Uzbekistan the cradle is called a* besjiek. *They are used in Uzbekistan, Tajikistan and Kazakhstan and Kyrgyzstan. A crosspiece, or* dasta, *connects the semicircular head end and foot end. In the bottom there is a round or hexagonal opening (tubak munak), under which a potty (tubak) can be placed. There are semicircular planks, jorga, that enable the cradle to be rocked. The height of these cradles varies between 50cm and 65cm, the length between 85cm and 100cm, and the width between 32cm and 42cm. There are round holes at the top of the head end and foot end into which a long turned pole, the kubba, is placed (in this illustration, however, the kubba is plain). Tajikistan 1972.*
[All photographs in this chapter were obtained through the author]

---

[2] In Nurata for example, an oblique cross was applied to a horse skull that was then impaled on a pole. This stood in the fields as protection against the 'evil eye'

[3] Millet was also thrown over the bride and bridegroom at their wedding in order to drive away malign spirits and at the same time wish well-being and many descendants on the couple.

the arms firmly against the body. This strap is then knotted to the crosspiece with ribbons. The legs are bound in a similar manner. A blanket or two cloths are attached to the head of the cradle with the help of the *kubba*, the long turned pole that projects from the cradle. The cloths are made from a variety of fabrics. It is probable that the patterns would have had a certain sacred significance in former times, but such information is not always easy to obtain nowadays. The meaning has, however, been preserved of the bedding belonging to the cradle, which is made from small pieces of fabric. This patchwork method is known almost everywhere in Central Asia. The technique and its product are called *kurok* or *kurama*.

Kuroki are amulets. The forms in the colourful patchwork have the characteristics of an amulet: squares or lozenges, or a cross constructed from these elements. The *kurok* technique is applied most often to objects that are used during moments in life when a person is

subject to the greatest danger from evil spirits, and is extremely important to rituals involving mothers and children: occult forces present an especially high degree of danger during the forty days following birth, the *chilla* period. Childless women may not visit the mother during this period, since the misfortune of childlessness is attributed to the influence of malign spirits. If the childless woman brings along a *kuroki* object, the visit is considered safe.

On important family occasions, such as weddings, funerals, the first laying in the cradle, or the first time the child's hair is cut, guests bring gifts of pieces of fabric. These are laid together, and afterwards an appropriate *kuroki* is sewn for specific family occasions. It is usual to attempt to get material for children and accessories for cradles from families with many and/or older children.

The cradle in the form of a hammock has a similar meaning. It is encountered in Turkmenistan and was called *sallanchak*, a term derived from the word *sallanmak*, meaning 'to hang' or 'to hang down'. The sallanchak was used in some regions of Tajikistan as a temporary cradle. Nowadays, it is only used in the Turkmen *yurta* or nomad tent.

The main element of the cradle is called *sallanchak kilim* and consists of a patterned napless double fabric. It is 100cm to 130cm long, and 60cm to 95cm wide. The fabric is tightly woven and waterproof. The *sallanchak* is hung so that the child's head is raised slightly higher than the rest of its body and any urine can run downwards. In order to prevent the child falling, it is bound with a strip of material or a cloth.

In order to improve stability, the sides are reinforced with sticks. Where possible, the sticks are fashioned from wood from the dagdan tree (*celtis causasica*), which grows high in the mountains. This wood is strong and durable, properties that, according to magical laws, are passed on to the child. The people of Turkme-

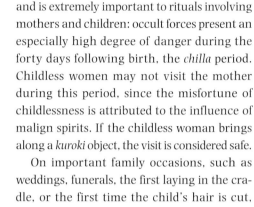

A fully dressed willow cradle, topped off with a turned kubba. The kubba is associated with the headdress, an important item of clothing, or with the heavens. In practice, the kubba is used to support drapes. These are hung over the head end and cover the cradle on two sides. Kazakhstan, 1991.

nistan regard the dagdan as a holy tree with protective powers. In contrast to other trees, it is free of spirits that could harm the child.

The *sallanchak* is secured by means of two long cords. Enormous significance is associated with these cords. They are twined using a particular method from woollen or cotton threads of contrasting colours – usually black and white. The cords are themselves amulets, and are associated with snakes. In Central Asia, the snake is seen as a talisman against death, the bearer of life-giving energy and protector against malign spirits. Turkmens and Tajiks embroider snakes on children's jackets and undershirts and a snake-head may be hung, as an amulet, from the cradle. A small bag of dried snakeskin or snake eyes is sewn onto the clothes of sick children. In Darbaz, in Tajikistan, new-born children receive a concoction of dried and ground snake tongue, snake eyes, butter and aromatic herbs. A snake can be used to cure infertility. The snake is involved in a wide variety of sacred practices that take place during the first year of a child's life.

The patterns on the *sallanchak* material are determined by tradition. The basic elements that form the patterns are the lozenge, with a dark or light central eye, in a complex 'horn' figure that is considered a talisman within Turkmeni ornamentation. White also has a protective function that is amplified by a contrast with dark colours. The pattern is composed of diametric stripes or diagonal stepped layers.

The motifs and pattern structure of the *sallanchak* fabric bear many similarities to those used on the funeral cloths on which the Turkmens lay their dead. The non-functional aspects of the hammock reflect centuries-old ideas about birth and death. This is also true of wooden cradles: they are made from the same wood as funeral biers.

A Tajik woman working with a child on her back. The underside of the upper clothing is folded over the child and the ends knotted at the chest. 1990.

The importance of the cradle for the child and its future is also expressed in a ritual that takes place when the baby is placed into it for the first time. This happens at varying times: sometimes five to seven days after birth, or in some cases fourteen or even thirty days later. It must, in any case, take place on the 'fortunate' days, Thursday or Friday. Until this time, the child lies by its mother on the floor. If the child is very restless, it may be placed into the cradle earlier. It is therefore thought that the cradle has a soothing effect on the child.

A new cradle is bought for the firstborn. The parents of the young mother must do this. If a *sallanchak* is required, the material is woven by the husband's mother (or in some groups the husband's oldest sister-in-law). The cradle may be passed on from older to younger children, especially if the children grow up healthy and strong. Should a child be sickly, the cradle is no longer used. However, it is not disposed of, because this may cause the woman to become infertile. An 'unlucky' cradle is usually brought to the burial ground or

A Turkmen grandmother in a yurta (nomad tent), rocks the sallanchak rhythmically back and forth with a long rope attached at one end to the hammock cradle and at the other to her big toe. Late 19th century.

with the possible exception of the comb – but are nonetheless often used in some Central Asian ceremonies and ornamentation as protection against evil. A broom means purity, and just like the *lepeshka*, it is the child's 'travelling companion'. The child must never be entirely alone, because malign spirits could then enter him, and that would be his undoing.

When the child is at last lying in the cradle, those present wish it good health and a restful sleep. The child's 'cradle period', which holds many dangers for its health, now begins. This period is extremely important to the child's future development. And it is for this reason that the cradle, and everything associated with it, is surrounded by large number of carefully formulated safety measures of a magical character.

Within each region there are local and ethnic variations on these measures. The practices relate not only to the child, but also to the mother; together they form a single entity for the first months of the baby's life. To a great extent, the child's fate depends on the purity of its mother and her protection against malign forces. The magical practices relating to the midwife and mother are as extensive as those relating to the child in traditional Central Asia. They have their own specific characteristics, but all serve the same purpose: the health and happiness of the child, and by extension the mother who thereby successfully continues the bloodline.

Depending on when the next child is born, a baby will spend between one and three years in the cradle – no longer than this, or it would stop growing. Europeans often think that this form of cradle can be damaging for posture and the shape of the head, and this view may

to a *mazara*, the place where an Islamic saint is worshipped (usually the grave).

Before the child is laid in it, the cradle is thoroughly cleansed with fire and smoke. A variety of incantations are spoken. Neighbours and family members – especially children and women – are invited to the party.[4] Food is prepared: *plov*, or pilaf; tea with sweets; and *lepeshki*, round biscuits that are broken and distributed among those present. Especially healthy women with many children are very welcome oft the party. Sweets and *lepeshki* are required fare, due to the powers attributed to them. A calm woman with many children lays the child in the cradle for the first time, but first a mirror, comb, whetstone, knife, red pepper, onion, garlic, a small *lepeshka* and the Koran are placed under the bedding. This collection of objects may vary according to subgroup. The mirror has a magical meaning. Some peoples of Central Asia regard the mirror as an attribute of the female deity, the goddess of the earth and of fertility. The stone provides the child with strength and power. The comb, knife, pepper, onion and garlic all serve to ward off evil spirits. They are all 'bad' objects –

---

[4] Some groups have cradle rituals with their own characteristics in various regions of Central Asia. In this chapter we are concentrating on shared practices. Furthermore, we have selected an isolated episode of this complex and multi-layered ritual. A separate chapter would be necessary for a complete description.

be well founded. The local population, however, believe the cradle to be a reliable way of ensuring that the child remains free of physical shortcomings. The thin mattress and cushion guarantee good posture, in their judgement. To ensure that the head does not become malformed, the mother gives first one and then the other breast when feeding; the child it is not removed from the cradle during nursing.

Wooden cradles can easily be relocated, indoors or out, but in doing so, the child's legs must not be pointed in westerly direction. This would be a grave sin. The *sallanchak* cradle is hung to the right of the entrance to the women's section of the *yurta*. Outside, it is secured to two poles.

In the early period of the child's life, it is removed from the cradle as rarely as possible in order not to disturb or overstimulate it. The *chilla* period is dangerous for both mother and child. The baby is not brought outside the living area or shown to strangers. Should this be unavoidable, it is wrapped in quilted blankets.

After the *chilla*, the baby is carried horizontally in the arms. If it becomes restless, it is placed vertically on the back and supported with the arms – this method of carrying is called *sardasti* in Tajikistan. If the child is able to sit, the adult has one arm free to continue working. In reality, however, the mother is unable to work until the child can walk. From that point the child is carried on the back. The underside of the upper clothing is folded over the child and the ends knotted over the chest. If the child is being carried in the arms, a sling is sometimes used. One end of the sling is wrapped around the child from above and the other end supports it from underneath.

The buggy is popular in modern Central Asia cities, and in modern houses, beds rather than cradles are used for children. In rural areas, however, the wooden cradle continues to be used, and *sallanchaks* are still hung *yurtas*. Traditional methods of childcare and traditional ritual practices persist in these areas.

Chapter 2.5.1

New Guinea

From the womb to the men's house

D.A.M. Smidt

Since time immemorial, women in New Guinea have carried their babies on the back in carry nets, just as they do the food from their gardens. Men also use carry nets, for example to keep cutlery or tobacco at hand; they are smaller than the women's, however, and the way they are carried is also different. Men carry

them with a strap over the shoulder or chest. Women prefer a strap around the forehead. Despite the advance of Western goods and culture, Papuan women still use the traditional carry net. It is not only a familiar sight in rural areas, but also in towns and cities on the streets and at markets. Nowadays, Western materials such as nylon thread, wool and chemical dyes are used in the production process.

The carry net is found throughout New Guinea.[1] Inland, especially at higher altitudes, it has always been part of local culture. It has only recently been adopted by the populations inhabiting low-lying regions along the rivers and the coast to the north, east and southeast of Papua New Guinea. The net was used in many places in the past, but not on the neighbouring islands east of New Guinea, where a bark-cloth sling is used. However, in the twentieth century the net was also adopted.

The carry net is inseparable from the people of New Guinea, from birth to death. They begin their lives in one – carried as babies – and sometimes their bones are buried in one. At important transitional events in life, such as birth, puberty, initiation, marriage and death, the carry net plays an important symbolic role.[2]

---

[1] Politically New Guinea is divided in two. The western half, Irian Jaya, is a province of Indonesia; the eastern half forms part of the independent state Papua New Guinea.

[2] A number of notable publications in the growing quantity of literature concerned with this subject have persuaded me of the significance of the carry nets in New Guinea – primarily a monograph by the Dutch missionary Father J. Hylkema O.F.M., who worked for many years among the Nalum inhabiting the Star Mountains in western New Guinea. It gradually became clear to him that the carry net was of great symbolic significance to both men and women. His study was entitled *Mannen in het Draagnet*, or 'Men in the Carry Net', and was published in 1974. A study published in 1991 by the English researcher Maureen Anne Mackenzie is especially important. It focuses on the significance of the carry net among the Telefol-speaking people's Central New Guinea, dealing in particular with the relationship between the sexes. For other relatively recent articles about carry nets as used by specific population groups we refer you to Christian Kaufmann (1986), who discusses the Kwoma inhabiting the Upper Sepik region; and to Gisela Schuster (1989) who describes the Central Iatmul of the Central Sepik region. The section of Paul Sillitoe's monumental work (1988) dealing with Wola carry nets in the Central Highlands also deserves special attention.

The carry net is the ultimate symbol for maternal care. Some bark, leaves or pieces of cloth are often placed in the net first. Sometimes the top will be covered with a banana leaf to protect against sun and rain. Measures are also taken to protect the child from malign spirits. The Arapesh do this by hanging bundles of magical leaves from the net.

The child is carried everywhere in the net. A woman returning from working in the gardens often has two nets on her back: the lower of the two, hanging at the upper thighs, contains the baby. Above it a large net hangs laden with agricultural produce such as tubers, sweet potatoes or bananas. By hanging underneath, the baby is protected from the rain, but reversal of positions does occur. The Kire have an unusual method of combining the various loads: the heaviest net is hung on the back and the baby is hung at the breast.

Carry nets are usually made in the village, either at home or nearby. This may happen in combination with other social activities such as sitting in a group, chatting. It can also be combined with cooking. While the baby or toddler is suckling, the women work on the net. Even when their work is heavy, they can use their rest breaks to for this activity; they even continue while walking.

Girls learn to do this from a young age. Among the Iatmul of the central Sepic region, girls as young as six or seven begin twining threads for their mothers and sisters. At a later stage, they are allowed to repair damaged areas of carry nets and fishing nets or help with a piece of the net that a sister or mother is working on. Only after having built up experience like this may a girl attempt to make her own carry net independently.

Net making is predominantly the work of women. Among the Wola, carry nets belong to the category of 'soft' objects at home. 'Hard' objects, such as axes and shields, are made by men. A male source noted: 'Women do only

the soft work. Anything requiring strength is men's work. Slow, easy work is only allotted to women.' However, an exception is made for the woman's head: 'Women do not have strong bodies. Only her head is strong.' With her head, she carries her children, firewood and yams.

There are nonetheless some communities, such as the Huli, where men produce their own carry nets. There is a strongly reinforced division between the sexes in Huli society, because the men are fearful that too much contact with women might be damaging to their health. Most Huli men live separately; they harvest their own sweet potatoes and cook for themselves. Some Kominimung men can, under their wife's supervision, repair the ceremonial carry net. (Sillitoe, 1988, p.557; 559)

The Wola operate a standard measurement for the quality of nets that is apparently accepted throughout New Guinea. The Wola

Papuan woman with two loads. Children are usually carried on the back in a carry net. Another means of transportation is the bark sling. The child does not rest on the mother's back, but lies under one of her breasts, which leaves the nipple within easy reach. Some Papuan groups use both the carry net and the sling. Nowadays, slings are often made from European fabrics. Abelam, Sepik Region, Papua New Guinea, 1971.
[All photographs in this chapter were obtained through the author]

All unmarried Wola women keep an unused carry net for the time it will be presented as part of the dowry. When this ceremonial net is dirty and almost worn out it will be used to carry loads. The presentation of a carry net marks the transition to womanhood in some groups, such as the Nalum. The Arapesh decorate girls with carry nets, among other things, after the first menstruation. In the Huon Gulf region, young marriageable women are required to cover their backs with one or two carry nets. As part of their initiation, young men living in many regions receive a special carry net with magical substances that will make them strong, wise and sexually potent. Elema boys' initiation ceremonies involve a ceremonial exchange between the uncle of the mother's side and his nieces and nephews. The uncle receives food and pigs. Nephews receive a bark cloth, a bow and arrow, and a carry net decorated with shell money. Nieces receive carry nets, also decorated with money. Traditionally shell money was used, but nowadays paper money is used.

Carry nets often serve as a means of expressing the relationships between social groups. This is most evident in the case of the net that forms part of the dowry. As part of the marriage ceremony, the bride-receiving group bestows a number of gifts on the bride-giving group. This is evidently a form of compensation, for the woman represents a considerable socio-economic value. It can also function as a seal on the new alliance between the two groups. The gifts are offered in a carry net. The bride herself may bring a dowry consisting of carry nets, which she presents to her sisters-in-law. But the carry net has already had a significant role in the individual contact between the two lovers: the woman presents the man with a net to indicate a favourable response to his advances.

Other life phases may also be marked by the use of a carry net, as in the Huon Gulf region. The older the woman, the larger the number

Older children are also sometimes carried in a net. Akrukay, Sogeram region, Papua New Guinea, 1976.

value the net according to yarn quality, stitch size and net size. Differences in quality occur because not all women are equally accomplished in the production of carry nets. Varying qualities of net are used for different purposes: higher demands, including aesthetic ones, will be made on a net intended for ceremonial use than on one intended for household use.

of carry nets that cover her back and chest. Elderly women are adorned with nets that hang to their knees. Melpa widows bear a black carry net on the back to indicate that the soul of the deceased husband has taken up residence in it. Around the Gulf of Papua, a widow wears a carry net containing her partner's possessions around her neck. To signify mourning, and after having, As a sign of mourning, Huli widows rub the head and upper body with grey clay and wear worn out old nets rather like a cape and veil.

In other regions the carry net is sometimes hung by graves, or at a specially constructed 'house of the dead' in which the corpse is allowed to decay. Sometimes the body is bound to a framework, consisting of two poles and a crosspiece, and put on display. It is then adorned with a carry net containing the personal possessions of the dead person. After the soft parts of the body have putrefied, the skull and bones are placed in the net. This is then hung in the communal building or stored in the sacred graves with the remains of ances-

This is a detail of the painting for the facade of a men's house. The two central heads of the mythical ancestors are nestling in an enormous carry net, represented by strips of triangular motifs. A row of white oval motifs can be seen just above the wooden crossbeam. This is a representation of the egg cowrie (Ovula ovum) shells attached to carry nets during ceremonies. See also page 114. Abelam, Sepik region, Papua New Guinea, 1987.

A young woman carrying a net to which egg cowrie shells are attached. She carries this during the women's dance that concludes a male initiation ceremony. This emphasises how vital women are for successful males. Abelam, Sepik region, Papua New Guinea, 1987.

tors. After removal from the death rack, the remains of deceased Nalum men are put in a net and kept for a time in the men's house before going to their final resting place in a rock face. Deceased women and children are represented in this ossuary by their almost completely decayed carry nets. Kwoma sons may keep one of their deceased father's bones at home in a carry net to ensure the continuing care and attention of his spirit.

The carry net also functions as a link between the world of the living and that of the ancestors, between the present and the mythical past. In the Central Highlands, sacred nets are kept in the most important men's houses. These are thought to be concentrations of supernatural powers that radiate over a large area. One might compare them with reliquaries: bones and skulls of important ancestors are kept in them, and these are sometimes accompanied by small personal items belonging to the ancestors, bundles of magical substances, and gourds containing the bones of animals consumed during ceremonial meals. The net may also contain the jaw of a totem pig or a piece of pigskin, and leaves and twigs. The net can serve as a deed of ownership, legitimising age-old territorial claims, possibly of mythical origin.

In some regions the carry net plays an essential role in the process of transition of the soul of a deceased to a newborn child. The Orokaiva associate this process with the land or garden that a person worked: after death, the person to whom the soul is transferred will continue to care for it. The deceased is solemnly assured of this during a ritual. The process of soul transition is lengthy. For several months the mother carries her baby in the carry net to the piece of land in question. She plants a stick into the ground, and from this she hangs the carry net. The soul of the deceased is petitioned to enter into the stick and subsequently, little by little, into the baby. In this way the crops in the gardens are nurtured by the soul of the deceased and the care of the living.

The value and associations attributed to the carry net partly depend on demographic and economic factors. Much food is produced in the densely populated Central Highland region, some of it for substantial ceremonial exchange with neighbouring groups. In this context, the carry net is mainly a symbol of the contribution of women to economic production. In more sparsely populated and less productive areas, the relationship between the carry net and female fertility and motherhood is emphasised (Mackenzie 1990).

It should come as no surprise that an object of such value is suffused with symbolism. The primary association is with the womb, for which the carry net is essentially an external surrogate: it can expand and contract, has similar flexibility to the walls of the womb and allows the child to take the same positions it did in the womb. The inhabitants of Umeda village in the Waina-Sowanda region in West Sepik use the term 'spirit carry net' for the womb (Gell, 1975, p.143). The similarity between a full and rounded carry net and the belly of a pregnant woman is striking.

In its function as a baby carrier, the carry net may also be compared with the pouch of marsupials such as the tree kangaroo or the cuscus. The Yopna use the same word (*yirk*) for both 'carry net' and 'marsupial pouch' (Kocher Schmid, 1991, p.152). In this context it is telling that some groups, such as the Baktaman, worship sacred marsupials. They are associated with the life-giving mythical ancestors and the taro tubers that form the basis of their diet.

It is not unreasonable to suppose that the material used for making the carry nets is chosen as much for its symbolic connotations as for its practical use. When fibres are used from the aerial roots of the pandanus palm – of which there are both male and female varieties – it is possible that there is identification with the feminine. Just as when a woman falls pregnant, her belly swells, her skin colour

Sometimes, a Papuan baby is temporarily 'parked': hung from a branch, the beam of a house or, as in this case, an uprooted tree trunk (the result of a river breaching its banks). A baby hanging in this way is a common sight. Kominimung, Ramu region, Papua New Guinea, 1977.

changes and her nipples darken, the pandanus also changes colour, its husks swelling until its fruit is harvested. Its aerial roots are reminiscent of elongated breasts, and especially the brown-coloured ends look like nipples. And lastly, as the breasts produces milk for the baby, the pandanus root produces the lightly coloured fibres from which the child's carry net is made. The carry net plays a conspicuous role in origin myths. Elements essential to the creation of life and culture are carried in the ancestral mother's carry net and distributed to their descendants. The primal carry net described in the myths is regarded as the prototype for all later models.

For both Umeda women and men, the carry net is an inseparable appendage of the personality: a doppelganger, soul or spirit. A man's net contains his personality in the form of his most personal possessions and some magical substances, while a woman's contains harvested food or her child. That a carry net forms part of the personality is a generally accepted notion: when, for example, one wishes to cause harm to someone using black magic, this can be achieved using a hair or a piece of a nail belonging to that person, but their carry net may also be used.

Papuan men are especially impressed by the ability of women to bear children. It is an event surrounded by secrecy. While menstruating or giving birth, the woman isolates herself. Anything related to the blood of women poses a serious danger to men. Menstrual blood is unclean and has potently polluting effects on the environment. This taboo is so strong that a father may not see his child for a period of several weeks or even months following birth – certainly not as long as the umbilical cord has not yet fallen off, because until that time woman's blood still clings to the child. It is believed that any Iatmul man that touches a midwife or a newborn child will instantly become old and weak.

It seems that the men have sought compensation for this exclusion. They isolate themselves in the men's houses where they organise rituals and make the artworks required for them. In their eyes, there are correspondences between the creation of art on the one hand and sexual intercourse, pregnancy and birth on the other. The Elema equate the making of an ancestral wooden panel in a literal sense with giving birth. The mythical ancestor is reborn, as it were, by taking up residence in the 'house', or panel, that the woodcutter creates for him. Before he begins, the woodcutter says a prayer directed at Mother Earth and the dead: 'I am going to bear the man who was born a long time ago' (Beier and Kiki, 1970, p. 280). The navel motif is central to the panels. It symbolises the navel that connects the clan to its founder, who is also depicted on the panel.

In the Sepik region, the men's house symbolises a mythical female creature in whose 'womb' young men are initiated into adulthood during a period of isolation equivalent in some regards to pregnancy. They are, in a sense, reborn. Here too, the appearance of a masked figure is prepared. Their emergence, the climax of the ceremony, sometimes reminds one of a birth scene. The men, therefore, have their own version of pregnancy and birth. Given the strong association between the male rituals and female fertility it is unsurprising that in a number of regions the apparently feminine attribute, the carry net, plays an important role in the rituals. Nets sometimes form part of the embellishments of mythical figures that appear as masked dancers. It also appears in the harvest altar of yams, at which the fertility of the land is associated with that of women. It also serves as a receptacle for sacred or ritual objects. The men sometimes adorn a carry net with shells before presenting it as a form of payment to the organiser of an important ceremony. The carry net also appears as a motif on carvings and paintings such as those in the ceremonial houses of the Abelam, where they refer to the primal mother's mythical net containing live elements like birds, snakes and stars.

The use of carry nets is widespread in New Guinea. They are of practical use in their many types, sizes and shapes, and are central to the lives of women. They are also laden with symbolism in the ceremonial aspects of men's lives. An object that at first sight is rather unspectacular elicits a huge variety of emotions and feelings among those who make and use them. Seen in this way, the carry net – which refers in equal measure to the mysteries of the womb and to the mysteries of the men's house – is no less fascinating than the sculptures or masks that have already been recognised as works of art.

Chapter 2.6.1

Lapland

The ideal cradle for travelling

N. Zorgdrager

Sami woman with child in komse. Lule Lappmark, Sweden. Lithograph from a photograph taken in 1868 by Lotten von Duben,
[G. von Duben, 1873]

The people known to many as Lapps are also called Fenni or Finnics in older literature. In their own language they are called Sami, and this has become the accepted modern name for them. The Sami live in the northern regions of Norway, Sweden, Finland and on the Russian Kola peninsular. They number approximately 60,000. Until the sixteenth cen-tury, they lived by hunting, fishing and reindeer herding. Both the farming societies of the coastal Sami and nomadic reindeer-herding cultures evolved from this way of life. Nowadays, only ten percent of the Sami population live a nomadic existence. In the nineteenth century, the Sami river-people came into being. They are fishers and cattle breeders who live in the inland regions of the Norwegian province of Finnmark and in northern Finland. A type of carry-cot called a komse, or gietkka in their own language, is common to all three population groups. This chapter looks at the use of this baby carrier among the reindeer herders, especially those in Finnmark.

The reindeer herders are nomads: during the winter they live in the inland woods, and for the summer they migrate to the Norwegian coast or the high mountains of the Norwegian and Swedish border region. Many of them lived the whole year round in tents until the Second World War. In the last year of the Second World War much of northern Norway was razed to the ground by the German occupying forces. Post-war reconstruction brought great changes. Increasing numbers of reindeer herders built wooden winter accommodation. However, even greater changes took place after 1970, when special home-building programmes were set up for the Sami regions. Modern houses were built – comfortable accommodation for both summer and winter. Nomadic reindeer-herding families could now travel back and forth between these two dwellings. The changes in the lifestyle of the Sami have also had their effect on baby- and childcare; the *komse* has increasingly fallen into disuse in recent decennia.

The basic design is a boat-shaped skeleton made from a hollowed out peace of tree trunk. It is between 65cm and 90cm in length and has a hood formed by two wooden bows at the head end. It is no more than 30cm in width and clad entirely in leather. The shape of the carrier, especially the hood, varies somewhat according to region: northern hoods are higher and rounder than southern ones. Variations in cladding also occur. The cot can be carried by means of a strap over the shoulder, or hung from a tent pole, a branch or the saddle of a reindeer used as pack animal. Other woven straps and a form of drape are among the additional elements that make up the complete baby carrier. The *komse* carrying strap consists of three narrow straps attached separately to the top and side of the hood; these are brought together to form a broader strap as they run down to the foot end. They are tied around the foot end in such a way that it is simple to loosen and remove the child from the *komse*. The patterns on the woven straps indicate whether the carrier contains a boy or girl.

The size of the *komse* was adapted precisely to that of the child, and as soon as the child outgrew one, a larger one was provided. The child would be carried in at least three before it reached the age of nine months. The smallest carrier was sometimes not used, but a fourth *komse* was often made for a slightly older baby. However, children older than eighteen months would seldom be carried in one except during the trek.

Nappies were not used; the baby lay on dried moss or moisture-absorbing powder – in more recent times an old absorbent piece of cloth would be laid over this. It also served as a mattress, and it covered the entire bottom of the carrier, but was thickest in the middle and at the foot end. The baby lay on its back on the hide of a very young reindeer calf or – at the coast – sheepskin. Its head and neck lay on the hairs from a reindeer neck covered with a woollen cloth, a down cushion or a hare or fox pelt. The child's feet were wrapped in a woollen cloth or reindeer hide. The fur on which the child lay was folded over it. When

Sami woman with a komse on her back. The drape has been pulled down to protect the child from mosquitoes and the sun.
[H.A. Bernatzik, 1938]

ever the child was removed from the *komse*, the mother would replace the moss. Soiled moss was burnt, but if it was only wet it would be dried on a reindeer skin outside in the sun, or over a fire in a large iron pan. In this way, moss could continue to be used until it was completely pulverised.

Very young babies lay with their arms at their sides; their only clothing was a close-fitting hat, which was originally made of fur, but later of wool. As textiles became more readily available, babies' arms and legs would be wrapped in old rags. Older children did not lie naked in the carrier – at least not from the twentieth century onwards. In addition to a reindeer calf fur jacket or woollen clothes, they also wore long woollen socks or trousers without a crotch.

Babies were generally born in the tent. The mother had already prepared the *komse*. A woollen hat would only be knitted after the birth of the child. The newborn child was immediately placed in warm water. It was regularly washed until the age of two. There were no nappies to wash because babies were naked and toddlers wore trousers without a crotch and with a large split front and back. When nursing the child, the mother would take the *komse* onto her lap. For this reason the hood of the *komse* could not be too high.

Although both men and women herded the reindeer, women with small children generally took no part in tending them. Most work they were involved in could be done in or near the tent. If it were nonetheless necessary to leave the immediate area – to chop wood or fetch water, for example – the baby was usually left in the tent; if the birch wood or water source was close at hand, the mother would not be away for too long.

If the child in the *komse* was awake, the drape would be pulled back and the carrier placed with the hood upwards in order that the child could look around. The *komse* was placed firmly on the ground or hung from one of the tent poles. Alternatively, the child could be rocked to sleep by pushing the *komse* to produce an undulating motion along its long axis. Many older writers note that this was different from the manner in which children of the same period living elsewhere in Europe were rocked to sleep: with a rocking or 'swinging' motion.

If the mother worked outside the tent during the summer, she often had her child with her. However, Sami women were fearful that their babies would be burnt by the sun, and so during periods of fine weather and few mosquitoes they were kept in the *komse* and protected from the sun by the hood and curtain.

The *komse* is praised in literature for its practical usefulness: the mother could carry it everywhere she went, and leave it anywhere too – on the ground, in a tree or even standing in the snow. O. Elgström, a Swedish artist,

observed this near a shop in Vittangi, when the mother placed the *komse* upright in the snow while she shopped.

The ease with which the *komse* could be transported was also extolled. The carrier could be worn on the back, hung at the side of a reindeer from its saddle or placed between the feet of the mother in the sleigh. It was an ideal cot to travel with – on longer journeys, trips to the market or church, or from one seasonal dwelling to another.

Distances of between 200km and 300km were covered during the autumn and springtime treks between the highland summer pastures and the winter grazing inland or in the woods. Both men and women lead trains, or *raids*, of reindeer in the trek. A *raid* usually consisted of six animals reigned together, in single file; when the leading animal was pulled, the others were forced to follow. If they were pack animals, it was very important that their load was balanced – not more than twenty kilograms on each side. The *komse* containing the baby always hung from the left side of the leading animal. On the right side, as counterbalance, a cooking pot, a sack of grain or sometimes a second *komse* would hang. Children not old enough to ride on a reindeer or walk independently would be placed in a *komse* for the duration of the journey. If two *komse*s were being carried, the lighter one would be weighted – with clothing for example. On occasion, the mother would carry the *komse* on her back. During extremely cold weather, the *komse* was wrapped in a covering made of the hide from the legs of white reindeer.

If there was snow on the ground and the trek was by reindeer sleigh, then the mother would have the covered *komse* in front of her on her own sleigh. If she needed to breastfeed the child she knelt next to the sleigh in the snow; she then only needed to loosen her woollen scarf, since traditional Sami clothing was put on over the head and had a slit at the front. Especially during winter journeys, a child could spend many hours in the *komse*, able only to move its head.

The *komse* was a safe haven; strapped in and with its head protected by the hood, the child could withstand a bump or two during a journey. A nineteenth century traveller said that on one trip he joined, a child was almost lost because its *komse* had been hung carelessly on the saddle and had fallen to the ground without the mother noticing. A travelling companion who happened to have remained slightly behind found the child, unharmed in the *komse*.

Just how safe the *komse* really was, however, is illustrated by events described by Frederick Rode, a Norwegian cleric who worked among the Sami in the nineteenth century. In Kautokeino, he once witnessed how 'a reindeer, harnessed to a sleigh containing a six-month-old baby in a *komse*, broke loose before the mother had stepped on, and disappeared like a shot into the wilderness.' The sleigh toppled over at the start of the reindeer's flight, and was dragged, upside down, over tree stumps and rocks. Rode continued 'It seemed reasonable to assume that there would be little left of the child's head, even before the reindeer had disappeared from sight. The Sami immediately began their pursuit on skis (...) it was only after five kilometres that the animal could be caught because the reigns had snagged in a bush and it could not move. The sleigh was turned over and the baby was found – fast asleep. The hood of the *komse* and the piece of material bound to it had absorbed all the jolts, and even prevented snow coming in.' And on Lake Leina in Sweden, an overladen boat was capsized by a strong gust of wind. All occupants drowned except for the baby; the *komse*, covered with leather, stayed afloat and was blown to shore.

The effective protection the *komse* provides was even a theme in a novel. In his famous book *Lajla* (1881) the Norwegian linguist and writer J.A. Friis tells of a *komse* being thrown

from a sleigh as a result of an accident. The *komse* rolls and rolls ever further downwards and finally lands on an ice floe drifting past the bank just upstream of an open waterfall. And so the Norwegian baby girl, Marie, who has been travelling through inland Finnmark with her parents in the traditional Sami way, is found by a Sami and grows up as the Sami girl Lajla.

In past centuries, the Sami bound a bow, spear and arrows – made of tin or reindeer horn – to a boy's *komse*, and the wings, legs and beak of a ptarmigan to a girl's. This was done in order to make the boy grow up to be a great hunter and the girl to be pure, skilful and quick. This custom probably disappeared during the eighteenth century.

To this day, a string of beads interspersed with rings and silver balls is hung from the straps of the *komse* for the baby to look at and play with. In historical documents, mention is only made of their function as a toy, but the beads, and especially the silver items, served another, equally important, function: they protected the baby against the *uldas* – beings that lived underground. According to Sami mythology, an *ulda* is a descendant of children of Adam. God visited Adam and Eve. Eve failed to wash all the children in time. She hid the unwashed children from him. When God asked if all the children were present, and Adam and Eve said they were, he said 'Those that are hidden from me, will also be hidden from humankind'

The Sami believed that the *uldas* were fond of human children – especially beautiful dark-haired children. When given the chance, the *uldas* would exchange a human baby for one of their elderly parents for whom they no longer wished to care, in the guise of a child. The switch could be made when the mother left her baby alone in its *komse*. The best protection against this were items of stamped silver. It was for this reason that silver balls and/or rings were threaded between the beads. Additionally, a flat silver knot was often affixed to the *komse* carrying strap itself, at the meeting point of the three narrow bands. Even when the child could walk, it often carried something made of silver.

In more southerly regions, both brass and silver were used for objects affording protection. Other methods were also used to keep the *uldas* at bay: baptism for example, provided good protection, and children were baptised early. A book of psalms, a prayer book or another religious work would be placed under the pillow of a child that had not been baptised. The inhabitants of these southerly regions where the first to end this practice; it survived longest in the north.

A child that had been swapped had a similar appearance to the parents' own child, but it did not grow well, did not learn to speak properly and it was more ugly. Such children (thought actually to be old men or women) did grow up, but they were different from normal children. Clairvoyants or dream interpreters could establish whether a child had been exchanged or not. The most effective method was to hit the child with twigs from a juniperberry bush until it cried hard. The *ulda* who had made the exchange could not bear to hear this, so came back to rescue the elderly parent, and return the stolen child. That such exchanges took place was an established fact among the Sami. They believed that children suffering from rickets or whose growth was otherwise dysfunctional were in all probability *ulda* children.

The Sami saw death as a dangerous force that also clung to the bodies of the dead. It was therefore considered inadvisable to come into any contact with a corpse without taking

A komse hanging from a branch in the summer pasture region in southern Troms/Ofoten, Norway. The komse is being rocked along its long axis.
[Photograph Wilse, 1916. Norsk Folkemuseum, Oslo]

Glass beads and silver balls hang from a komse carrying-strap: not only toys, but also protection against malign spirits.
[Photograph E. Manker, 1953]

precautionary measures. People kept as far away as possible from corpses and brought them quickly to the mortuary at the church. Anything that had touched the deceased was burned or thrown away, whether it was a sleigh on which the body had been transported or a *komse* in which a child died. Elgström wrote 'At the bottom of the hill behind the church at Karesuando there always lie discarded blankets, sleighs, hides and sometimes a cradle.' Each spring, the sexton pushed the discarded items into the river. If a *komse* was not use to transport a dead child to the church, it was left where the tent was pitched to indicate the spot that was not to be used again for this purpose.

In earlier times, it was not considered harmful to strap the baby tightly into the *komse*. According to outsiders that journeyed there, babies seldom cried once strapped in. What is

the opinion of the modern medical profession on the use of the *komse*? Have they encouraged or, for some reason, discouraged its use? Unfortunately there is little material to be found on this subject.

In 1931, a doctor named Kloster published a paper on rickets in Finnmark. The number of cases varied fairly widely from settlement to settlement, while the communities all had similar diets: mostly fish and some meat. Only in one settlement was the population predominantly Sami, and reindeer breeders were not among those selected for the study.

Rickets is caused by a deficiency of vitamin D in the diet, combined with a lack of exposure to the ultraviolet rays of the sun. Kloster noted 'a horror of fresh air' among both the Finns and Sami, but nowhere does he refer to the *komse*. Rickets cannot, however, be caused by non-exposure to sunlight alone. Reindeer-breeding Sami protected only babies from the sun; as soon as they were able to walk and leave the *komse*, they spent much time outside. As far as I know, no studies have focused on their diet. Nonetheless, Rickets did occur among the reindeer breeders. If a child displayed clear symptoms of the disease, it was indication among the Sami that it had been 'exchanged'.

A commonly observed birth defect among the Sami is congenital hip luxation, which causes a limping gait. Doctor B. Getz was in no doubt that the position of the baby in the *komse* contributed to the further development of the hip misalignment, although this was not necessarily the primary cause. The increasing availability of medical care, and the growing number of Sami women giving birth in hospital since the end of the 1950s, has made it possible to diagnose this defect at birth and to treat it.

Nowadays, Sami mothers are aware that strapping a child into the *komse* is not conducive to its physical development. However, the main causes of the decline in use of the *komse* are changes in the lifestyle of the Sami. Women no longer travel with the whole family on the spring and autumn treks with their herds. They take the children and any household goods and clothes they require from their inland winter accommodation to their coastal settlement for the summer. The mountain villages in which Swedish Sami spend their summers are often accessible by boat. The tents and cabins formerly used by the whole family have been replaced by comfortable modern homes. Only during the trek itself do they still live in tents. And when selling souvenirs, many families occupy tents during the daytime.

Methods of transportation have also drastically changed. The use of the reindeer as a pack animal disappeared in 1950s. The snow scooter, introduced in the 1960s, has made the herders more mobile. This has led to the development of central villages with shops, medical facilities and suchlike. As the women

and children joined the trek less frequently, so the use of reindeer sleighs declined. They fell into complete disuse in the early 1980s. Anything that must be transported across the wilderness is pulled on a sleigh behind a scooter.

All these developments have also had their effect on baby care. Sami children wear baby clothes and cellulose nappies, and lie in a bed or buggy. One sees a baby in a baby carrier only rarely. The *komse* has become an heirloom, a decorative object in the living room. The few mothers that do still use the *komse* have only one, and only place their very young baby in its during the daytime so that it is safe on a couch at home or on the back seat of a car. Thus, the *komse* nowadays has a similar function to a pram without wheels; and what is a pram after all than a wider and somewhat larger *komse* on wheels.

A komse. There are leather or sometimes cotton flaps that overlap when pulled across to cover the child. The child is tightly packed in, up to the chin, by threading a 3m-long leather belt or woven strap crisscross through leather loops attached to the sides. The mother secures one end to the foot of the komse, and one end to its head. It is attached in such a way that she can remove one end without loosening the other. In this way an older child could occasionally be allowed freedom of movement of the hands, or moss could be changed without removing the baby. The komse carrying strap consists of two or three narrow bands that are attached to the hood and converge on their way to the foot end. The drape used to be made of tanned leather, but nowadays is made of cotton with floral designs.
[Photograph, N. Zorgdrager]

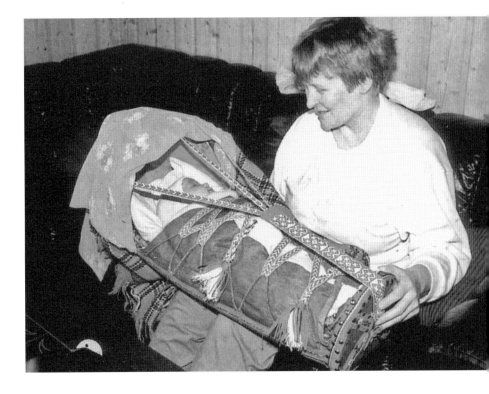

Chapter 2.6.2

Siberia

Safe and sound in a micro-house

K.J. Solovieva

In traditional Siberian society, great significance is attached to the notion of family. To remain single or childless is to invite disapproval. An expectant mother receives special attention in accordance with an entire system of protective measures and regulations, as does the child during its early development. In this context, the child's cradle is of great significance. Each population group has its own rituals and practices that apply to the baby carrier itself and the period in which it is used.

The carry-cot is one of the most authentic and consistent expressions of traditional culture in Siberia.[1] Almost all indigenous cultures there use it in some form. Only the Inuit carry their children in a bag made of animal hides or fabric. There is large amount of documentation available – more than thirty distinct population groups inhabit Siberia – but it is impossible to discuss in detail here all types of baby carriers and associated rituals. For this reason we will restrict our study to the Ugric peoples of Ob, the Khanty and the Mansi.

A decorated daytime cradle made of birch bark hangs from a pole by two long straps. Khanty.
[K. J. Solovieva, 1988]

---

[1] The term 'traditional culture' refers to a culture characteristic of a societal form existing around the turn of the 20th century – one that revolves around industry, family and daily life. In this chapter, use is also made of more recent ethnographic material in reference to traditional practices that have been preserved, such as those relating to childrearing.

The Ugric peoples of the Ob have long been established in a vast region of West Siberia in the Ob river basin. Reindeer breeding is the predominant occupation of the Northern Khanty and Mansi peoples, and they live a largely nomadic existence. Handiwork is characteristic of the eastern Khanty, who live in permanent settlements.

Especially to the north, there are generally few children in each family. This is largely a result of the harsh environment, a severe climate and epidemics, which naturally make an impact on family life. The behaviour of family members is clearly regulated, and is related to certain perceptions of their surroundings. It is believed, for example, that the natural world is inhabited by benign and malign spirits who are in constant conflict with one another over the fate of humanity. For this reason, the baby carrier has not only a practical function, but also a symbolic one.

Ugric peoples have a variety of baby carrier designs, and these are made according to certain guidelines. Among the Mansi, women – usually the mother or another female family member – make the carrier; among the eastern Khanty, men make the day carriers, while women make the temporary carriers and those used at night.

The temporary cradle (*niavram caz*, or, literally, child container) is a plain square basket of birch bark closely resembling the basket used around the house by many Siberian peoples. There are openings at the bottom of the cradle and straps are threaded through. These are used to tightly bind the arms and legs of the child. Sometimes straps are only attached at the sides. In summertime, a bow made of bird-cherry wood is attached to the carrier to support a drape. The temporary carrier is generally not hung up. During long tracks, it is placed in a special reindeer-hide bag with an opening that facilitates breastfeeding. The Khanty child remains in the temporary cradle until the umbilical chord has fallen off, but a Mansi

When travelling short distances Chantis and Mansis take the carrycot in their arms. On longer journeys, the carrying straps are thrown over the neck and the cradle rests against the abdomen. Sometimes the cradle is carried on the side or back, with the straps over the shoulders. Evennen, eastern Siberia, early twentieth century.
[All photographs in this chapter were obtained through the author]

child continues to lie in it until it is three or four months old.

The Khanty and the Mansi believe that Anki Pugos, the 'giver of life', is the mother of newborns. Secretly and invisibly she exerts her influence on the child. Thus, it is thought that the child is connected with an invisible being for an initial period – the end of which could be signified by the umbilical cord falling off or healing, the first smile, or the appearance of the first tooth. Children who die during this early phase are buried separately to preclude any danger of it turning into a *patsjak*, a being that hounds people and strikes fear into them. It appears that in the period that the child enjoys the protection of Anki

Ostjak woman.
[Pokrowski, 1882]

Pugos, the parents neglect certain aspects of childcare. Only after the child begins to recognise its mother is it seen as having been released from the supernatural world. These notions are doubtlessly bound up with the high rates of mortality in early infancy. During this period, many rituals and sacrifices take place that involve pleas for a healthy and long life for the baby.

According to the Ugric concept of the world, the soul of a deceased family member takes up residence in a newborn when the child receives a name. The ritual proceeds as follows: a knife is placed in the temporary cradle; an older, female family member lifts it up while the others present say the name of the deceased person; the cradle is placed on the ground; and from this moment the child has both the soul and the name of the departed family member. The child is later told the identity of the person whose name it bears. In this way, connections with the ancestors are preserved.

Before a child is placed in the permanent carrier it is first washed with an extract of *chaga* (a fungus that grows on birch trees), and the carrier is fumigated with smoke. The Mansi carrier is made of decorated birch bark while that of the Khanty may also be made of birch or cedar wood. The permanent carrier exists in two forms: one for daytime use and one for night-time.

Although another woman may make the night cradle, it is usually the mother that does so, prior to the birth. It is approximately 80cm long, 30cm wide and 15cm high. It is oval and slightly wider at the head end. The underside is made of two layers of birch bark. The sides are attached a little way in from the edge. The bottom is trimmed with a strip of reindeer hide. Loops are sewn into a strip of reindeer hide at the sides and at the foot end, through which straps are threaded. The pillow in the cradle is filled with soft wood shavings or reindeer hair. The bottom of both day and night cradles is strewn with pieces of rotted birch wood, which is very absorbent. Soft hair or reindeer wool lies on top of this; moss with disinfectant properties is sometimes added. This litter may also consist of pieces of reindeer hide or the skin of a diver waterfowl. A round or oval canvas, woven from birch bark and trimmed with a dark fabric, is wrapped around boys' hips to prevent the blanket being soiled. The blanket for a newborn is made from the skin of twenty to twenty-five duck heads, or alternatively from the skins of swans or hares. Older children are covered with reindeer skin.

The Mansi and the Khanty from the north make their day cradles from birch bark and then decorate them. The oval base is attached at right angles to the perpendicular head end. Cedar roots are sewn on the inside with sinews to achieve the correct shape. Two large straps are attached to the sides and head end for carrying or hanging. Additionally, a bow of bird-cherry wood or a purple-willow twig is attached, over which a protective curtain or cloth is laid. Carved ornamentations on the sides and head end are created using a scraping technique. The rear of the head end is divided into horizontal and vertical areas, and the sides into only vertical areas. Different ornamentation is used for boys' and girls' carriers. The head end of a boy's cradle is entirely covered with decorations, while a girl's is only carved at the top. A bird is always depicted on the upper part: the Mansi use a black grouse and the Khanty a capercaillie. They believe that the soul has the form of a bird that can leave a person, especially when they are asleep, thus exposing them to danger. According to an alternative tradition, birds fly *towards* a sleeping person.

It is the men of the eastern Khanty who make the wooden baby carriers. The wood used for it is selected with great care. Particular attention is paid to the distance between the cedar tree rings; these must be at a certain distance from each other for the wood to be considered 'correct'. The base and back of the

cradle are attached to one another at an angle of 120°. The base is a semi-oval, and at the head end two circular panels meet in the middle. The sides are made of bowed cedar planks. Reindeer hide, usually from the head, is attached to the upper part of the head end for protection. Alternatively, a small bag containing the umbilical cord may be attached, or a cross carved into the board. The cross, symbolising fire, protects the child from evil.

Birch and cedar trees are sacred, and this is why their wood is used for cradles. The birch is connected with a higher realm, life and the sun. This 'good' tree exerts its special power

The carrycot used by a child that has died is hung in a ' burial tree', often a cedar.
[Tobol Gouvernement, Mansen, 1909-1910]

over malign spirits. The birch is also of enormous practical importance because it is easy to work, resists moisture and maintains a constant temperature. *Chaga*, the fungus that grows on birch trees, has antiseptic qualities and is therefore a good natural medicine for many diseases.

The day cradle is used both for the child to lie in during the day and for transportation over longer distances. It can be hung from special hooks and a chain carved from wood; the chain is between 70cm and 80cm long, and the hooks at each end have small pegs cut into them that create a calming ticking sound when the cradle rocks. Eastern Khanty men sometimes carve the hooks from the bones of reindeer or elk and engrave decorations into them. Iron hooks have also been used. The hooks gain a sacred significance from the material used to make them. The elk is considered an ancestor by many groups, the reindeer is a useful domesticated animal that is often sacrificed to the gods, and iron has protective powers.

Evennen, eastern Siberia, early twentieth century.

The birch bark or wooden day cradles are light and easy to carry. The carrier with a child in it is no heavier than a child in a blanket. The straps and the relatively high sides prevent the child from falling out. The angle at which the head end and base are attached to each other allows it to be hung from any branch.

If the child's time in the cradle passes successfully, the cradle will then be used for any subsequent child. In this way, children are connected not only by sharing the same house, but also the same cradle. The carrier may not be thrown away, broken up or sold. If children are often unwell, or die, a 'successful' carrier may be borrowed. A carrier that belonged to a deceased child is hung in a tree, often a cedar.

A child spends the first year of its life in the carrier. Even when being breastfed, the child is not removed from it. The cradle is seen as a

micro-house with protective powers that are amplified by talismans and amulets. In principle, the child is never left alone until it has its first teeth, but if for some reason it is unavoidable, the tip of the child's nose is sometimes rubbed with soot. It is more usual, however, for the parents to light a fire and ask it to protect the baby. Nowadays, a box of matches will be left behind: fire is the most powerful charm against evil.

The bear is one of the most physically powerful animals, and thus it determines human existence to a large degree; as well as being a totem, it is the protector of home industry. Thus, bear teeth and nails have the power to ward off evil spirits. The beak of the black-throated diver has a similar effect. These objects are hung from the rear of the cradle. A knife or a stone with an unusual shape may also serve as an amulet. Waste from the cradle – the absorbent rotted birch wood, which must be replenished frequently – may not be disposed of under a tree because, according to local tradition, the child would grow up to be weak. The child's clothing is its amulet from the moment it leaves the cradle. Bells are sewn to it as protection against malign spirits. This also allows parents to find the child more easily if it is out of sight.

Toys play an important role in a child's early interaction with the surrounding world. A low-hanging string of beads, pendants and bells is attached to the cradle, parallel to the semicircular bow supporting the curtain. Goose necks or swan necks filled with small stones, or bladders containing berries and needles, serve as rattles. Capercaillie feathers, reindeer bones, tails, homemade textile dolls and wooden capercaillie or reindeer may also be used as toys. Children must also become accustomed to the harsh climate from an early age: mothers sometimes wash their children in the open during very cold weather, lay them in the sun with their head unprotected, or rub them with snow.

The traditional baby carrier is a characteristic miniature dwelling. It is also a symbol of fertility and welfare. It indicates something of the child's age (temporary and permanent cradles) and gender (decoration and shape). A 'fortunate' carrier ensures good health and wards off external interference. The consistent and intricate system of rituals and practices associated with the cradle, and its rational design, underscore the special significance this object has to the lives of Siberian peoples. The baby carrier is closely linked to a traditional view of nature and is an expression of the relationship between humans and the natural world.

Chapter 2.6.3

Greenland

A wide sealskin hood

B. Robbe

Greenland Inuit women and girls usually carry babies and small children on the back in the hood of a specially made garment. It is made in a variety of styles, either of caribou hide or sealskin, depending on the region. In this chapter we will concentrate largely on this type of clothing worn by the Kalaalit and the Tunumiit, who live on the east coast of Greenland. In their language, Tunumisut, the garment is called an *amaarngut*. This is derived from the verb *amaarpa* which means 'something on the back, against the back, to carry something wrapped'. The word indicates the means, method, and the instrument: the *amaarngut* is a garment for carrying something on the back. It is worn during the summer both indoors and outdoors, and over other clothes during the winter. The description of this garment, and the socio-cultural phenomena associated with it, is based on observations we made in 1969 in the Ammassalik region on the east coast of Greenland.

The *amaarngut* in which the baby is carried is made of sealskin and is worn with the fur on the inside. The outside is more or less white, depending on how it has been used. The garment is relatively short: it reaches to above the thighs at the sides and ends in a point at the front and back, at the level of the crotch. Its width at the hip and at its lowest point is roughly equal, but it becomes significantly wider on the back: here it ends in a wide-open hood.

The *amaarngut* is pulled over the head. To do this, the woman bends down with her arms stretched forwards. Sometimes it can be quite difficult to fit the narrow lower part of the garment over her shoulders – especially since the arms have to slide into the sleeves at the same time – but with some acrobatics it is possible

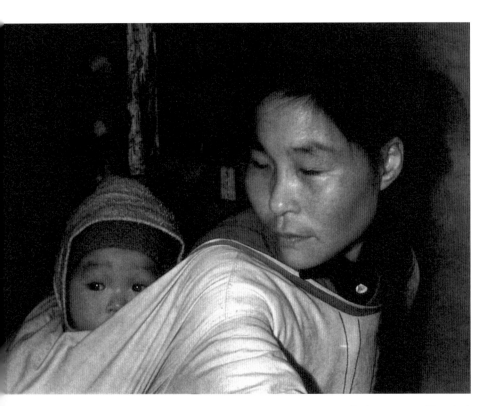

On the east coast of Greenland.
[Photograph B. Robbe]

to get the *amaarngut* into place. The woman's head appears through the opening without trouble. This is pulled to one side of the neck and over the opposite shoulder.

A long strap, attached to the *amaarngut* at chest level with a reinforced seam, is passed under the arms, wrapped around the body and tied again at the front, thus forming the bag in which the child is carried. By changing the height at which the strap is tied, the size of the bag can be altered. A piece of bone or ivory is usually knotted at the end of the strap so it can be found more easily to undo the strap in an emergency.

The *amaarngut* is made from two sealskins: one forms the hood and the back, and the other, the front. The underside of the sealskin is used for this purpose. The sleeves are cut from the upper part. Narwhal or seal sinew is used as thread. The back, which is broadest at the shoulders to provide freedom of movement, is attached to the front piece by a seam that runs around the shoulders and ends as a tab at the edge of the front of the hood at shoulder-blade height. This method spreads the child's weight equally over the seams – and the skin in general – ensuring that the garment remains in good shape. The seam is decorated where it ends on the chest. Generally, this is a narrow band of light-coloured short-haired fur from the legs of a dog or from an *ilimeq*, a young seal. This describes the main characteristics of the *amaarngut* but many design variations are possible depending on what skins are available.

The back of the *amaarngut* can be made wider or deeper according to the needs of the growing child or the wishes of the mother. The garment may be cut and sewn by the baby's maternal grandmother (especially for the first child), or other female family members. The mother usually makes it, however, from her second child onwards.

The sealskin is selected for its suppleness, short fur, and sturdiness. The Inuit use skin

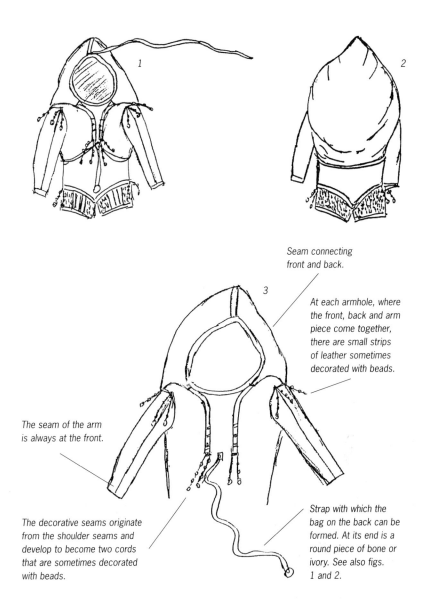

Seam connecting front and back.

At each armhole, where the front, back and arm piece come together, there are small strips of leather sometimes decorated with beads.

The seam of the arm is always at the front.

The decorative seams originate from the shoulder seams and develop to become two cords that are sometimes decorated with beads.

Strap with which the bag on the back can be formed. At its end is a round piece of bone or ivory. See also figs. 1 and 2.

Drawing by B. Robbe (1971) of the front (figs. 1 & 3) and back (fig 2) of an amaarngut.

Explanation of the illustrations:
1: With a strap attached to the top of the hood, the wearer can pull the hood over herself and the child, or only over the child.
3: A leather connecting-piece reinforces the seam just in front of the peak of the hood, where the hide is thinner (the seal's head).

[Photograph B. Robbe]

from three types of seal: young hooded seals, young harp seals, and leaner adult ringed seals. The *amaarngut* is always made from two skins of the same species.

During the winter, the Inuit wear another garment, called the *tatuulaq*. It is similar in design to the *amaarngut*, but its hood is wider. It is worn with the fur on the outside. These two garments fit together in much the same way as Inuit boots, which are made up of an inner and outer layer. The *tatuulaq* is made of larger and thicker skins than the *amaarngut*. The skins are used either of young bearded seals or adult harp seals.

Nowadays, it is common practice to use the word *amaarngut* whether this garment or the *tatuulaq* is being referred to. The *tatuulaq* is in any case becoming increasingly rare. Nowadays, it is only worn indoors, without the *amaarngut*.

The child is pushed feet-first through the neck opening and laid carefully on the mother's back. When alone, the mother pulls the opening to one side on one of her shoulders then, leaning the shoulder slightly forwards, she lays the baby onto it, on its stomach. Formerly, the child was naked from the waist down – indoors it was often completely naked.

Today, *amaarnguts* are usually made of white cotton or coarse white linen. They are often decorated with beads, and the hood, sleeves and skirt are edged in red. They are worn in both summer and winter in the villages and where the Inuit store their tents. Children are no longer carried naked: they wear light or warm clothing according to the season. The design of the garment remains unchanged, however.

The *amaarngut* is an expression of the continuity of life. The concept of a possible renewal of life is closely associated with the garment. Girls, and sometimes boys, wear an *amaarngut* from an early age. Adult women always wear one after the birth of their first child.

Girls care for babies from the age of nine or ten. They may be asked to take a baby for a walk in an *amaarngut* belonging to their aunt, sister or mother. The way the girls, and sometimes the boys, carry children, made a great impression on me. They exude a mixture of pride, tenderness and earnestness in addition to a sense of responsibility. We should not idealise the situation – the same child may have been angry when its mother disturbed its playtime or sleep in order to take care of the baby – but when wearing the *amaarngut* and carrying the child, they seem suffused with dignity. And this is indeed the case, for they are fulfilling a role provided for them by their community. They participate in an activity that is a sensitive issue because of its vital importance to the group: the protection and nurturing of life. The living being lying against them, and their responsibility for it – even if only for a short period, allows them to build up a relationship with life. They come to understand the fragility of life, the complete dependence of the youngest children and their need for help and protection, without needing to resort to words. And the girls understand what their role is: to fill the bag on their back.

Adults will often approach a child carrying a baby and say something pleasant. Sometimes it will be given a sweet, a coin, a sandwich or something else the adult happens to have at hand.

In Inuit communities, pregnancy is a period of both spiritual and physical danger. This danger is at its peak during birth. Delivery is not experienced with the same feelings as the carrying of the baby. There is a refusal to become emotionally attached to the unborn child, which as yet has no name and thus does not exist. This is a rational approach considering the high death rate of both infants and mothers during delivery. Any bond would prove to be an extra handicap for any mother whose entire reserves of mental and physical energy are required merely to survive in the harsh living conditions.

The *amaarngut* is actually a continuation of the womb, both for mother and child. The mother now lives with the child and can enjoy it in a way that was not possible during pregnancy. She can feel its movements – its heartbeat and breathing – on her back. She can keep it warm and feel its warmth. In effect, the pregnancy continues. And in temperatures that can be problematic for all newborns, the *amaarngut* offers the necessary protection.

Inuit children are introduced gradually to the harsh outside world: the low temperatures and the snow are dangerous for a baby, as is the cold air it breathes. The Inuit make sure when the child is taken out of the *amaarngut* that its face in particular is protected. This is not just to prevent its face from freezing, but most importantly to stop icy air from reaching the lungs directly. On its mother's back, the baby breathes air warmed by her body, and is protected from contact with the cold outside air by the animal hide or fabric. There is thus no abrupt transition for the child when the mother leaves the house.

The younger the child, the better it is protected. The very young baby lies on the mother's back almost as it would in a hammock. When it is bigger, it will more or less sit upright on the back. The hood, whether raised or not, protects the child and prevents direct contact with the cold. The child also often wears a hood itself The *amaarngut* enables the mother to watch over her child. She feels its body warmth, she can be sure that it is not cold, she feels its reactions and movements: she can be sure that it is alive.

Children are carried in the *amaarngut* until they can walk. But also after a child can walk, it may be moved in this way, depending on the circumstances, the distance to be travelled or the means of transport. But until the child can walk, it spends almost the whole day on its mother's or a family member's back. If the child cries it will be taken out. The mother leans forwards, shifts the child sideways over her back and lifts it by holding it under the armpits, then pulls down the wide neck opening so she can breastfeed it. While travelling, the mother can feed her child without removing it from the *amaarngut*: she takes one arm from its sleeve by pulling it backwards, then slides the child under her arm – this is possible because the back of the *amaarngut* is so wide. She can then nurse the baby with its head in the warm hood.

When a child needs to urinate, or has already started, the mother takes it out in the same way. She holds it between her knees, and if there is no snow on the ground or pot available, she cups a hand to catch the urine– it doesn't matter if it overflows. During long journeys, the soft and supple skins of young seals, or pieces of old but soft clothing, are laid under the bottoms of very young children, together with moss and lichen. If the *amaarngut* gets wet anyway, it is turned inside out and scraped clean and wrung later in the day with the child has been taken out. A little water is sometimes used to rinse away the urine. When it is dry, the *amaarngut* is made supple again by rubbing with the hand.

To calm the baby, or get it to sleep, the mother rocks her upper body to and fro. Meanwhile she performs the daily chores, talks, or sings a lullaby. If the baby is very restless or cries often, it may want to get outside. This is when a child may be asked to take it outside in the *amaarngut* and walk around for a while.

During boat journeys the child lies protected and out of harm's way in the *amaarngut*. Because the mother does not have to watch out for the child, she has freedom of movement. Women row *umiaks* – boats between six and twelve metres long that are used for whale hunting, migration and summer journeys – while their babies sleep on their backs, rocking back and forth to the rhythm of their mothers' movements.

Part 3

Detail of a baby sling with loop decoration, Nigeria. This is a decorative sling to be worn over a normal one.

Esan woman with her baby in a white lint cloth. Ewatto, Western Nigeria.
[Photo B. Menzel, 1992]

Weaving loops and tufts

Chapter 3.1

Techniques in Nigeria

M.A. Bolland

The woven fabric in which the child is carried may be a plain length of fabric, but usually it is embellished with decorations similar to those found on garments worn by the general population. On Java, batik fabrics are therefore used for this and many other purposes, and in Guatemala striped woven cloth is used both for slings and wraparound skirts. West African babies are carried in the same cotton or hand-woven fabrics worn by their mothers.

The Tropenmuseum in Amsterdam has four Nigerian baby slings worn as decorative cloths over the normal sling. They are between 170 and 200 centimetres long, and between 35 and 50 centimetres wide. They feature central decorations, extending from selvedge to selvedge, created with either looped or cut-looped tufts. In the original English-language descriptions, the cloths are referred to as 'tufted' without always clearly differentiating between the two forms. In her book *Nigerian Handcrafted Textiles* Joanne B. Eicher specifically mentions the use of cut tufts for the baby slings used in Zria, and looped tufts in the decorative slings of Bida and Ilorin. She claims that the cut-tuft fabrics are generally used by important people: those in eminent positions at the Awujale court, members of the Ogboni fellowship,[1] and chiefs on Owo. They wear a tufted fabric as 'medicine cloth'. Cut-tuft fabrics originating from Ijebu-Ode, which was an important centre for weaving in the past, are called *saki*.

The book *Nigerian Weaving* by Venice Lamb and Judy Holmes includes a number of illustrations of both types of fabric, which, it is explained, play important roles during rituals. They are woven especially for members of the Ogboni fellowship. For this reason, a central area of tufts is reserved for special magical powers that ward off potential danger.

Whether the looped tuft or cut tuft technique is used, if the cloth is intended for ceremonial use it is called *shaki*. They probably originated in Ijebu-Ode. The indigenous herbal doctors wear a *shaki* over the shoulder. Both looped and cut-tuft fabrics are made intensively in Igara; nowadays they can be found throughout Nigeria. Judy Holmes believes that the cloths probably originate in Igara irrespective of the market where they are sold. Lisa Aronson writes that these fabrics were still being intensively produced by female Ijebu

---

[1] The Ogboni Fellowship plays a key role among the Yoruba. Membership is not secret, but non-members may not attend meetings or rituals. All important and spiritual leaders, including a number of influential female elders, are members of this fellowship. It is responsible for all aspects of community affairs. Details from Hans Witte.

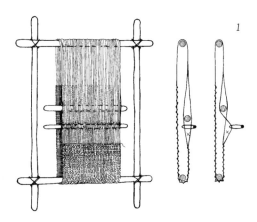

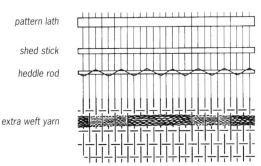

pattern lath

shed stick

heddle rod

extra weft yarn

weavers in 1978, usually for colourful wraps worn during important events.

Little is known of the weaving techniques used. In this chapter we will therefore further investigate the production of the tufted fabrics. The description is based on the study of the decorative fabrics in the Tropenmuseum collection.[2] One of the cloths has no tufts, but, judging by the finishing of the edges of the shorter sides, it was probably produced by the same woman who made the other two baby slings. It interesting to investigate how the particular striped effect is created by the alternation of the coloured thin and thick yarn in warp and weft.[3]

The weaving of tufted fabrics is women's work. Holmes calls an upright loom an 'Igara loom' after the area in which it is used. In Judy Holmes' book there is a photo of a statue erected in honour of the weavers of Ore. This life-size artwork depicts a woman at her upright loom; the already completed fabric is probably decorated with cut tufts.

The women of West Africa weave on an upright body-tension loom (see fig. 1). The warp threads run around two horizontal sticks and thus form an area of vertical yarn. The weaver sits on a low stool in front of her loom and, using the shed stick and heddle rod, works the weft threads down one by one between the front warp threads. All even warp threads go

Weaving a baby carrying cloth decorated with loops. The weaver is working on a row of loops. Ododo weaving centre, Okene, Kogi State, Nigeria.
[Photo B. Menzel, 1992]

---

[2] The technical data arising from the research into these five pieces is supported by the findings of Dr Brigitte Menzel. My thanks to her for permission to use her notes for the final section of my article.

[3] Baby slings from the Tropenmuseum collection: series 4325, numbers 5, 6 and 41. They were purchased in Aran Orin in Kwarra, a federal state of Nigeria, by H. Leyten, Curator for Africa at the Tropenmuseum, while on an educational trip in 1977. Series 5314 numbers 1 and 2 were bought by Mrs Amadi in Ibadan, Nigeria, in 1990.

The weaver loops the thick weft yarn around an auxiliary rod. Ododo weaving centre, Okene, Kogi State, Nigeria.
[Photo B. Menzel, 1992]

over the shed stick, and all odd ones under it. The thick shed stick, which is often made from a part of the midrib of a raffia palm leaf, creates an opening between even and odd warp threads. The weft thread shuttle is passed through this space from left to right. This is the first weft. The second weft is performed with the heddle rod. The heddle rod is a palm-leaf midrib; it lies on the warp, and loops of fine rope or yarn hang from it. Each of the odd warp threads passes through one of these loops. From the perspective of the weaver, the heddle rod is underneath the shed stick. The weaver raises the heddle rod, lifting all the threads running under the shed stick above the area of even warp threads. In this way a second opening is created through which the shuttle with the weft thread can again be passed through from left to right. These two actions are continually repeated. In order to increase the openings created by the shed stick and heddle rod, a wooden slat, the sword, is pushed into the opening and turned on its side. The sword additionally ensures that the most recent weft is securely pressed against

the already completed section of fabric. By means of this simple instrument, the warp thread is usually made more noticeable in the resulting fabric than the weft thread.[4]

A simple way of introducing decorations is to use warp thread of varying colours. Because the warp threads dominate, this creates coloured stripes running along the length of the cloth, in the direction of the warp thread. Joanne Eicher believes that these vertical stripes help the weaver determine where the woven motifs should be placed.

An alternative method of creating decorations is to incorporate extra weft threads. These are thicker and have a contrasting colour, and are repeatedly passed over a number of warp threads (see fig. 2). On two of the slings in the collection (4325-6 and 4325-41) it is possible

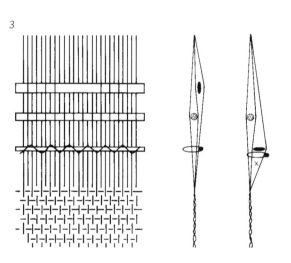

3

---

[4] Many factors, including tension and yarn thickness, affect the visibility or dominance of each of the two threads in fabrics made using the 'linen weave', whereby the warp and weft threads are crossed – one up, one down. Space is too limited to discuss this in detail here.

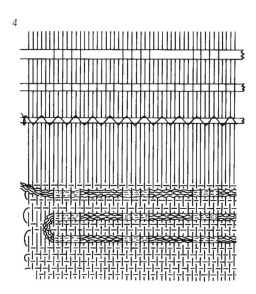

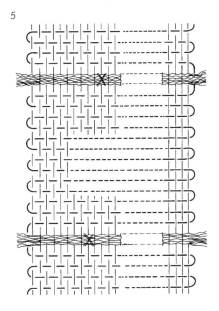

to discern how a pattern lath (a palm leaf midrib) has been passed through the warp threads above the shed stick – four threads over, and four threads under (see fig. 2 and 3). The following method is used to weave on these weft motifs: two wefts of the basic weave – one using the heddle rod the other using the shed stick. With the help of the pattern lath, a weft is woven with the thick yarn used for motifs on a contrasting colour such as blue. This is pressed firmly into place over the previous weft with the sword. It is followed by two wefts of the basic yarn and then one of the decorative yarn, and so on.

The short blue lines formed by the thicker decorative thread are positioned next to one another along the whole length of the piece; they each go under and over the same warp threads. It can therefore be concluded that a device would have been constantly placed in the warp during the weaving process: the pattern lath. In this way, stripes may be formed that extend from selvedge to selvedge (known as the *lancé* technique) as well as two or three decorative wefts and simple isolated geometric shapes. Each motif is created by a separate thick thread running from side to side (*broché*). The transition from one extra weft to the next occurs on the good side of the fabric; this applies to both the lancé and the broché techniques (see fig. 4). Because these additional wefts are passed over the original basic weave – achieved using the shed stick – they can hardly be seen on the reverse side.

The cut tufts that decorate items 4325-6 and 4325-41 are applied in a similar way. In both cases, the same warp threads pass over the tuft thread and so grip the double standing tufts in the weave throughout the cloth. Little can be seen of the tuft thread on the reverse side of the fabric. This also suggests the continual use of the pattern lath.

All of the baby slings feature lancé and broché motifs and cut-tuft wefts. To create them, there must have been a pattern lath in the threads running over the shed stick: over four and under four. Each tuft weft consists of a bundle of coloured threads with a knot. The knots are positioned on the right-hand selvedge (the way in which the tufts are created and the function of the knot will be discussed later). The decorative cloth 5314-2 features looped tufts and no lancé or broché motifs. Here too, a pattern lath was used to introduce the loop thread. The pattern lath was used somewhat carelessly during the making of this piece however: it is usually passed under four warp threads, but at other times over three or five. The number of warp threads running under

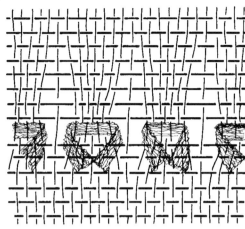

the pattern lath varies from five to seven.

The tuft yarn consists of a bundle of threads of the same colour, either white, orange, purple or black, which run from selvedge to selvedge. If the pattern requires it, the tuft yarn turns at the selvedge, on the good side, and forms the next row of tufts in the opposite direction. The threads are, therefore, extremely long. The knot is missing from one end.

The loops form square or rectangular areas in the large central area of the cloth. They alternate between black and white or orange and purple along its breadth. The two loop threads come together here through the same opening between the warp threads. One coloured thread forms loops and the other forms short lines under the rows of loops. In only one black and white row do the two threads not pass through the same opening between the warp threads. There is one weft and the basic thread between them. A number of transverse rows have areas with and without loops. In the areas without loops, the two thick threads form small crossing lines. The distance between the rows of loops is three, five or seven wefts of the basic thread, which is equal to between 0.5cm and 1cm. For the cut-loop cloths mentioned earlier, the distance varies between eleven and seventeen wefts, or 1cm and 2cm.

The cut loops in the white sling (5314-1) were woven using an entirely different technique. The thick white decorative thread runs along the length of the piece, and although it is a distinct thread it is not an additional weft thread: it replaces the basic thread at every fourteenth weft. In all probability the weaver made the cloth in this way: the first thirteen wefts of the basic thread followed by a fourteenth weft with the decorative thread projecting from both selvedges. During this weft, the tuft thread was pulled out to form loops (see fig. 5).

Figure 6 shows how the cut pieces of tuft thread are each held in place by seven warp

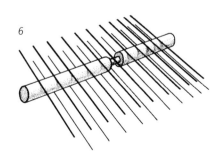

threads. The thickness of the two projecting ends serves to firmly press the seven threads against each other. This creates a kind of slit, or opening, in the fabric, running along its full length, narrowing down until it disappears almost completely at the next tuft weft thread.

Looking at these slits, it is possible to see that the tuft weft thread is not always pulled to form a loop and cut above the same warp threads (see fig. 5). Nonetheless, the cut loops are ordered fairly regularly above each other, and they generally do not vary by more than one or two warp threads. This strongly suggests that a device placed in the warp determined the positioned at which the tuft thread should be pulled to form a loop.

Joanne Eicher describes the looms on which the cut tuft cloths were woven, but not very clearly. She writes of a pattern lath in the warp with narrow notches through which every sixth, eighth, tenth or twelfth warp thread passes, depending on the number of threads between the notches. Figure 7 shows how this might have looked. The pattern lath is positioned above the heddle rod and between the warp threads in exactly the same manner as the shed stick.

This unusual pattern lath may well have been used as follows. Using the heddle rod, the thick decorative thread was laid between the warp threads. They now followed a weft using the pattern lath with notches instead of the shed stick. Because of the notches, the sixth, eighth tenth or twelfth warp thread was repeatedly lifted slightly lower at regular intervals. The weaver then knew that the decorative thread running over the warp thread had to be pulled into a loop at this point. It is possible that the pattern lath sometimes shifted, which resulted in the wrong warp thread indicating the position for a loop. Alternatively, the weaver may have been somewhat careless. This also resulted in the slit not always running between the same warp threads.

All five decorative slings – four with looped or cut tufts and one without – have a fringe of loops of warp threads at the short side. The fringe of sling 5314-1 is 3cm long, and this is its only finishing. In addition to fringes of between 6cm and 8cm, the other carriers have closed edges made using the weft ply weave (see fig. 8). For this weave, two threads – usually of different colours – run from selvedge to selvedge. One thread passes over and under a group of warp threads while the other passes under and over the same group, causing them to cross repeatedly. This method is also frequently used for basketwork.

The baby sling 4325-5 has no tuft decoration. It nonetheless belongs among the decorative cloths because of the spectacular effect achieved by the variations in colour of the warp threads in combination with the application of thin and thick weft threads. In this fabric, the weft threads are entirely covered by the warp threads, which run in vertical stripes 3cm to 3.5cm in width. They alternate in colour between light and dark blue, or yellow and dark blue. Figure 9 illustrates a small part of a vertical comber unit. The warp threads form small staggered lines by a darker warp thread and then four times a dark and a light warp thread. This is repeated. Four fine and two thick weft threads are alternated. This results in the thin and thick crossing lines, which are five warp threads in width.

During an educational trip in the spring of 1992, Brigitte Menzel bought a loom and two white slings for the Tropenmuseum – one with looped tufts and one with cut-loop tufts. The weaver parted with her body-tension loom when she was halfway through the eighth row of loops. The cotton continuous warp is 48cm in width and 205cm in circumference. There is a pattern lath between the shed stick and the heddle rod, and this is threaded 'three over/two under' in the warp threads running over the shed stick. These three aids, all made of palm leaf midribs, are always present in the warp.

The rows of loops always follow after a weft using the shed stick. The sword is put on its side in the opening made by the pattern lath. The weaver removes as much of the thick loop thread from the bobbin as she needs for one row of loops. She pushes the bobbin into the opening past the sword and pulls the thick thread through until it is flush with the opening. She then picks the thread up where it passes over seven warp threads and lays it in a

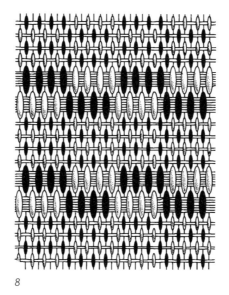

8

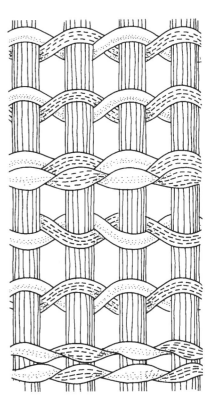

9

loop over an auxiliary rod (see fig. 10). She continues to work her way from selvedge to selvedge. The thread is not cut. After weaving one centimetre, she pulls the auxiliary rod from the row of loops and makes the following row in the opposite direction.

The loom, and the fabric made on it (155cm long and 50cm wide; Tropenmuseum collection, no. 5509-2), was bought in the Ododo weaving centre in Okene, in western Nigeria. The weavers, Ebira women, explained that the craftswoman herself decided whether the loops would be cut or not. This was done with scissors after weaving was complete.

The white cut tuft synthetic cloth (120cm long and 42cm wide; Tropenmuseum collection, no. 5509-3) is from the Igara. As with the previously mentioned cloth no. 5314-1, the cut-tuft thread replaces the basic weft thread.

The Ododo weavers said that the Igara loom also has a pattern lath in the continuous warp.

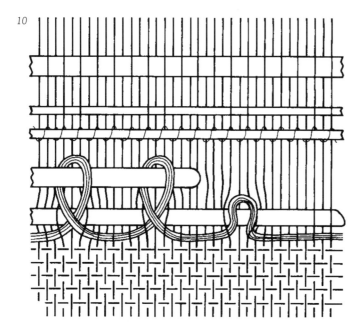

10

The importance of yarn

Chapter 3.2

Techniques in Peru

E. van der Hoeven

Inti (sun)

The art of weaving in Peru is thousands of years old. Bags, baskets and mats were already knotted and woven there from around 6000 BC. The most ancient fragments of cotton fabrics were found during excavations at Huaca Prieta on the north coast. Many of these were buried with the dead; they are dated at c. 3000 BC.

The discovery of these soft cotton fibres at the coast, and the wool of llamas, alpacas and vicuñas (a local species of camel), gave a major impulse to weaving activity, which was boosted even further by the introduction of the loom between 2000 BC and 1400 BC. Weaving developed from this time in pre-Colombian Peru. A technical and artistic peak was reached during the Paracas period (c. 1200 BC to 400 BC). All later techniques are known and were applied from this time: warp and weft rep, tapestry, gauze and mesh fabrics, kilim, double

fabric, embroidery appliqué en feather appliqué. Mats for roofs, blankets, fishing nets, shrouds for mummies and clothing were made during this period.

The weaving tradition persisted during the ensuing Moche, Naska, Tiawanaku, Wari and Chimú periods; the final great blossoming was the vast production that took place during the period of the Inca Empire, between 1458 AD and 1532 AD. Textile was crucial to Inca society. First and foremost, textile was the most important indicator of status. A person's place in the community could be identified by the clothing they wore. *Kumpi*, a delicate and exclusive fabric made of vicuña wool was reserved for the Inca family and the most senior nobility, for example, and *awasqua*, a simpler and rougher material, was used by the general population. These are only two of a many variations in quality associated with certain social groups. Possessing textile was also a form of capital ownership: woven fabrics that could be presented as gifts were kept in storage. Textile also had an important ritual function: the dead were buried in costly fabrics many metres long.

Moreover, textile played an important economic role. It was the accepted currency for trade and the payment of taxes. To achieve the high level of production required, the authorities enforced the textile *mit'a*, the obligation of subjects to weave for the state.

Following their conquest of the region, the Spanish forbade the weaving of *tokapus* (symbolic motifs) and the use of Inca garments. The local inhabitants were compelled to dress according to Spanish custom. Clothing has remained largely unchanged in the Andes region since colonial times. Men wear trousers, shirts and jackets made of *bayeta*, a sheep's wool fabric woven by men on a pedal loom – both the type of loom and the sheep were introduced by the Spanish. The remaining elements – poncho, belt and the coca pouch, which survived from the traditional indige-

Before the weaver begins her task she offers a number of coca leaves (at her feet in the photograph) to Pachamama (Mother Earth). She does this to ask for the strength to complete the difficult task successfully. She will often also tie a thread spun anticlockwise around her wrist as a protection against evil influences, and to safeguard against laziness.

[Photograph E. van der Hoeven]

the breast beam and the warp beam, between which the warp threads are stretched in a figure of eight. The simplicity of this loom, which has nonetheless been a source of aesthetically superb and technically exceptional fabrics since pre-Colombian times, has defined the most important characteristics of traditional Andes textiles: because of the continuous warp threads on the breast beam and the warp beam, the textile produces four selvedges. One result of this is that the fabric is complete when removed from the loom; the dimensions must therefore be determined before weaving commences.

The width of the loom is influenced by the length of the weaver's arms, which means that fabrics created on them are usually no wider than 45cm to 60cm. For this reason, larger garments, such as ponchos, baby slings and decorative cloths always comprise two woven halves, or *khalu*. These are in principle identical, and after completion, they are sewn in mirror image to each other with an ornamental stitch.

This technical detail is related to *Yanantin*, the ideological principle of duality, which plays a fundamental role in the cultures of the Andes. The two halves are seen as male and female, and the prevalence of this theme is

nous costume – are usually woven by women from alpaca wool on the four shaft loom.

A similar contrast is seen in the costume of women: skirt, blouse and jacket are made of *bayeta* (baize) in Spanish style, but the belt, coca pouch, baby sling and decorative cloth are woven in the traditional manner from alpaca wool or even sheep's wool. Nowadays the use of synthetic yarns is increasing, however.

In the Andes region of southern Peru, baby slings are usually woven on a horizontal heddle and shed stick loom. This consists merely of four stakes knocked into the ground: the front and back pairs are joined respectively by

Quollur (star)   *Q'enqo (canal)*

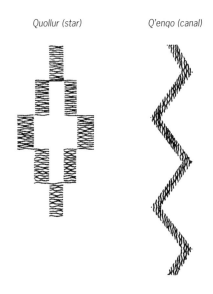

T'ika (flower)

Chakra (cultivated fields)

illustrated by the use of ritual slings, *unkhuña*, which, although smaller and woven as a single piece, are nonetheless divided into male and female halves.

The weaving of larger pieces usually takes place in the dry season between harvesting and sowing, from June to September. When weaving, a woman sets up the loom on her land, perhaps helped by her daughters or a neighbour to prepare the warp threads. She must already have decided the exact colour effects and decorative motifs for the final design, as these are partly determined by the number of warp threads. Alpaca wool is preferred for the warp and weft threads, since it is the strongest and warmest available, and is highly valued. Where alpaca wool is rare and therefore expensive, sheep's wool or a combination of the two is used. Whatever the yarn, it must be very strong, elastic and tightened to equal tension. This is necessary because of the nature of the weaving technique – picking up warp threads to weave in the motifs, *pallay* – and because the weft thread is driven home with a llama bone or vicuña bone, *wich'una*. In order to obtain such a strong yarn, the weaver will

often ply it twice and then wind it into a ball, sometimes around a stone.

In contrast to the more usual S-spun or twined yarn (twisted to the right), Z-spun or twined yarn (twisted to the left) is usually used in the weave for magical purposes. Mourning ponchos and decorative wraps, for example, have narrow strips of S-threads alternating with Z-threads to ward off malign spirits. The same applies to decorative wraps and baby slings made for special occasions such as weddings or the birth of a child. A herringbone motif, *lloq'e y paña* (left and right), results from the way in which light is reflected differently from the S and Z threads. The integration of *lloq'e y paña* into important fabrics is an application of the *Yanantin* principle.

A local saying '*Tambien el hilado es de hilos*' (literally, 'also the yarn is made of two threads') clearly refers to the duality principle, and emphasises the importance of yarn to the weaving process.

The technique described above of picking up certain warp threads with the point of a small stick creates a figure in the warp, called *pallay*. This method of decoration, sometimes in narrow strips, sometimes covering the entire piece, is characteristic of the weaving art of the southern Andes region.

Qocha (lagoon)

Wood and leather

Techniques in Lapland

N. Zorgdrager

In earlier times, all Sami men and women knew how to make a *komse* for their children. They needed no drawings or manuals to do so. Descriptions by Scandinavian experts were written for interested outsiders; Ossian Elgström, who came from Karesuandolapparna, wrote one such publication in 1922. Gunvor Guttorm's book *Gietkka*, however, which was published in 1991, was written in Samic for a Sami readership. As a textbook for high school craft lessons, it aimed to pass on to children the skills of their elders.

Traditionally, both men and women are involved in the making of a *komse*. The men produce the woodwork: the shell and the bow for the hood. Wood from birch, poplar, pine or spruce trees is used. Pine is easiest to find in the extreme north, but poplar is lighter.

The best tree is a dead, but not decomposing, pine – it is then unnecessary to take into account the effects of drying while the wood is worked. Should it be necessary to fell a living tree, this takes place when the moon is waxing. The wood is then stronger, and easier to work. A piece of the trunk without side branches is selected for the carrier. This must be a metre long and between 35cm and 40cm wide. It is then split in half lengthways. Nowadays, a power saw is used for the initial, heaviest, work. The head end is rounded with a saw. Sawing straight cuts into the inside makes it easier then to hollow it out with an axe. After this rough work, the wood is left to dry in a cool environment for several months. At no point, even during subsequent working, must it be exposed to wide variations in temperature. After drying, the shell is worked with a plane, gouge or other scraping implement, until the shell walls are approximately 1cm thick at the head end, and 1.5cm for the main body of the cradle. It is essential during this process to achieve the curvature leading to the head end that gives the *komse* its characteristic boat shape. The smallest *komses* are 65-70cm in length on the inside; the head end is 27-30cm wide and the foot end 15-17cm wide.

Karasjok and Kautokeino *komses* generally have a separate support at the foot end; it is attached to the side walls and is significantly

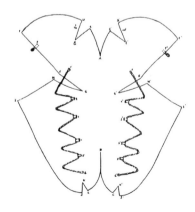

Pattern to make a Komse.

higher than the sides. In southern regions, this support is integrated into the shell, while to the east it is entirely absent.

The bow support for the hood is made of birch, willow or bird-cherry wood. Pieces are again selected that have no knots or branches. This wood must not dry out. The bows are 65cm long, 3cm wide and 7mm thick. These dimensions, especially the length, may vary according to region, however, since not all hoods are equally high or rounded. The bow shape is achieved by securing the wood in clamps or by creating the required tension with a cord attached at both ends. At a distance of 22-25cm from the middle of the head-end, notches are made in the head end and the sides of the shell, through which the end of the bow are 'piaited'. The bows are secured to one another at the peak of their arches with sinew or nails.

A *komse* is extremely durable, but traditionally a new leather sheath would be provided for each new infant. Women perform this work. A dried reindeer hide is attached loosely at the foot end, it is then pulled over the shell and head end. Here it is cut into shape. It is then removed and the hood is sewn. The seams, especially those over the backward-facing bow are often reinforced with a strip of leather – to which further decoration is sometimes applied – or a strip of baize. The hood is then pulled onto the framework once more and the remaining material is pulled towards the foot end. Cuts are then made for the seams to the left and right of the hood and at the foot end. The seams are then sewn closed. In Karesuando and Kautokeino, the side pieces that are closed over the child are made of leather and are integrated into the sheath. In Karasjok, these are made of fabric. Two metre-long twined leather cords are attached along the sides of the *komse* skin so they each form five large loops through which crossing straps will later be threaded. The casing is then soaked, pulled over the *komse* framework and the last flap is

folded inside the hood and sewn. When the leather dries, it is stretched tightly over the carrier. When the leather dries, it is stretched tightly over the carrier. The maker of the *komse* will already have taken into account the attachment points – usually loops of twisted leather – at the foot and head ends for the 'sleeping strap' and at the head end for the 'eye cloth'.

There are three methods for making the *komse* strap, or 'sleeping strap'. It sometimes consists of two parts: one strap 3.5-4cm wide and three narrow bands, all of the same width, which are sewn on – this bond may be reinforced with red baize. Alternatively, the strap may be woven in one piece, whereby the broad part is made first, then later the warp threads are divided to form the three narrow bands. Lastly, three separate narrow bands may be woven: they are sewn together at one end by stitching a piece of red baize around them. This is repeated at the point at which they separate.

The whole process is explained in detail in Guttorm's book. She also supplies the weaving patterns used by the Karasjok and Kautokeino for straps. Although the book was written with the intention of maintaining cultural knowledge, its publication may also be seen as a signal that the *geitkka*, or *komse*, belongs to a dying tradition.

A split leaf as a tool

Chapter 3.4

Techniques in New Guinea

D.A.M. Smidt

Traditional carry nets in New Guinea[1] are made using thread made from natural fibres. These are obtained from trees, bushes or vines that grow in the wild, or from trees or bushes cultivated for the purpose. The vegetation used varies from region to region. Fibres are often gathered from the inner bark of preferably young trees. Some groups, such as the Kominimung, use fibres from the aerial roots of the pandanus palm.

The pandanus can develop gigantic aerial roots. The men hack them off and carry them to the village, where the women set to work on them. They cut a notch in the bark, and then tear off a strip about 2cm wide, giving access

to the inner root. Strips of fibres are removed in the same way. The women split these fibres and remove the membrane around them. The resulting fine threads are rolled backwards and forwards over the thigh. When a bundle of threads has been made, work can begin on the carry net.

The production technique can best be described as knotless looping. No weaving, braiding or knitting takes place. The mesh stitch used in knitting, for example, is essentially different from the loop stitch used for carry nets. You can completely unravel knitting by pulling on the thread, but this is not possible with a carry net.[2]

Traditional carry-nets are generally made without tools. However, in a number of areas it is customary to use certain aids. In the central mountain region, for example, spacers are often used made of strips of leaf or halved leaves. This ensures that the loops are of equal size. When a spacer is used, the loops are made around it. Inhabitants of the Sibil valley in the Star Mountains make the stitch horizontally around a strip of pandanus leaf. Where no spacer is used, the thread may be wound around a finger – usually the index finger – to determine the size of the mesh.

The Wola use, among other things, a split leaf. On completing one row of stitches around the leaf, the maker of the net holds a second leaf of the same size parallel to the first and makes the second row of loops contiguously. Each stitch is made by threading the yarn to one or two loops of the previous row of loops. The loops transfer from strip to strip. This process continues until a rectangle of about two dozen rows has been completed. The maker may work from left to right and turn the net over as she completes each row, or, if

---

[1] Politically, New Guinea is divided into two parts. The western half, Irian Jaya, is a province of Indonesia; the eastern half is part of the independent state Papua New Guinea.

[2] My thanks to Rita Bolland for her clarifying comments on techniques.

she is equally skilled with both hands, she may choose to work alternately from one end to the other. When the carry net is big enough, she makes rows of loops that gradually increase in size. The carrying strap is formed from about ten of these longer rows. On completing the right number of rows for the carrying strap, the maker folds the net in half along the middle, so the longer ends lie one over the other. She then pulls out all the spacers. A few stones may be placed in the bottom of the net to achieve the right shape before the seams are sewn up. (This process is described in more detail in Sillitoe, 1988.)

As much as 430m of thread may be needed to produce a carry net of 75cm by 50cm with a 2.5cm mesh. A carry net of average size may be produced by a Wola woman in around 30 hours. However, it takes twice as long to prepare the yarn. Annually, each woman makes between 20 and 30 carry nets; a quantity that evidently satisfies only traditional needs. There is no evidence of increased production arising from commercial considerations. If a husband put too much pressure on his wife to produce more nets, this could have the opposite effect: she might leave him and return to her family.

A geometrical pattern is usually integrated into the net, using dyes. There are three steps to this process: the dye is collected and prepared; it is applied to measured lengths of the twined yarn; and finally, the coloured and uncoloured yarns are combined to create the desired pattern. For example, when the rows are made so they go up and down in steps, partially crossing over one another, a pattern results of varying horizontal coloured strips and a chequerboard effect in which the colours alternate in the diagonal. The Kwoma, for instance, make nets in this way.

Generally, a distinction can be drawn between the motifs applied to nets for everyday use and those reserved for ceremonial occasions. Nets that the Iatmul used for carrying

Twisting rope. Kominimung, Ramu region, Papua New Guinea, 1977.

[Photo D.A.M. Smidt]

ticular dye is unavailable. In some areas there are patterns only on the front of the net, as with the Kwoma. In other areas there are generally identical patterns on both sides, as with the Kominimung.

This carry-net is being shaped using coconuts. The geometric patterns are in two colours, and represent a praying mantis. Kominimung, Ramu region, Papua New Guinea, 1979.
Foto D.A.M. Smidt

firewood are coarsely meshed and decorated with a simple striped pattern. The bags the women use for small household objects and stimulants are also simply decorated. Ceremonial carry nets, however, are finely meshed and decorated with complex patterns. Only women above the age of about eighteen can make these richly decorated nets.

The patterns on ceremonial carry nets are usually geometric. Straight strips or bands, curved bands, zigzag bands, triangles, lozenges, squares, rectangles and crennelations are common. The lozenge motifs on Iatmul carry nets are often made with two colours, while zigzag motifs have three: the natural colour of the raw fibre plus red and black. If another colour is used, it is not as an addition but rather as a replacement – for example if a par-

Part 4

Six ways to carry children

D. van Buren and A. Vons

Cradled across the breast or on the hip in a Javanese *slendang*

Many Javanese people in Indonesia carry their children in a *slendang* at the hip. The *slendang* is fastened with a twist on one shoulder, without using a knot. Children are sometimes put to bed together with the familiar sling to reassure them. The *slendang* method is used for babies and children aged up to three or four. Babies lie in the sling; toddlers sit on the hip.

1. Take a cloth measuring about 2.10m by 90cm (7 by 3 feet).

2. Lay the cloth over one shoulder. At the front the cloth should hang down to your stomach.

3. Pick up the child and lay it diagonally across the cloth against the uncovered shoulder.

5. Lift up the child and the cloth a little. Twist the end of the cloth round twice from the neck towards the shoulder.

4. Bring the cloth that is hanging down your back forwards under the armpit on the uncovered side. Lift the end of the cloth up to your covered shoulder.

6. Take the piece of the cloth that is still hanging over your stomach and pull it tight. This will securely tighten the twist at the shoulder.

The European version of the *slendang* method

In Europe there is a variant of the Indonesian *slendang* method, using the same cloth. The difference is that with the European technique the cloth is knotted. The knot can be left in place for months at a time; as the child grows bigger and heavier, the knot has to be moved. Like the Indonesian version, the European *slengdang* is used for babies and children up to the age of three or four. Babies lie in the sling; toddlers sit on the hip.

2. Lay the cloth over one shoulder. Tie it at your hip with a reef knot.

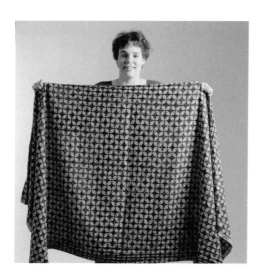

1. Take the cloth measuring about 2.10m by 90cm (7 by 3 feet).

3. Turn the cloth by pulling until the knot is between your shoulder blades.

4. Lift the child into the sling from above.

6. Spread the cloth over your shoulder from your neck, then seat the child in the sling.

5. Place the child on your hip and lift it up a little so the cloth lies loosely on your shoulder.

High on the back in a woven Andean cloth

In the Andes Mountains children are carried on the back in warm, woven cloths. Babies are first swaddled, while bigger children sit unrestricted in the cloth. In this way the children are carried long distances to market or work. Babies are wrapped up entirely in the woven cloth; the arms and legs of bigger children are left sticking out.

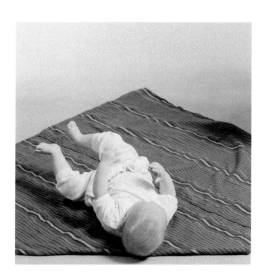

2. Lay the cloth down and fold back one corner. Lay the baby on the cloth.

1. Take a cloth measuring about 1.50m by 1.50m (5 by 5 feet).

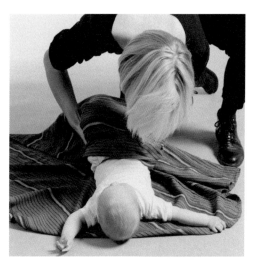

3. Tuck in the legs: take one corner of the cloth and tuck it under the baby's bottom.

4. Take hold of the cloth close to the child's neck, with your arms crossed.

6. Tie a reef knot across your chest.

5. Turn the baby around onto your back: keeping the arm underneath clamped to your breast, lift the other arm around over your head.

7. Spread the cloth over your shoulders and stand up.

On the back, in an African cloth over one shoulder

In Africa people nearly always carry children on the back, also when they are working in the fields, on the market or in the house. When the baby is breastfed, it is brought around to the front under one arm, then returned to the back afterwards. Children are carried like this from when they can first spread their legs until they are three or four years old. Babies have their legs and arms inside the cloth, toddlers have their arms and legs free.

2. Bend over forwards. Lay the child on your back with its legs apart.

1. Take the cloth measuring about 2.10m by 90cm (7 by 3 feet).

3. Lay the cloth over the child. The top edge of the cloth is at the level of the child's neck. Tuck the legs in.

4. Pull one end of the cloth tightly over your shoulder.

6. Spread the cloth over your shoulder and chest. Stand up straight.

5. Pull the other end of the cloth forwards under your armpit. Tie a reef knot at collar bone level.

On the back, in an African cloth with two knots at the front

With this technique from Ghana the children also sit on the back. When they are small, the cloth covers their arms and legs. From the age of one, the arms and legs hang outside the sling. The Ghanaian method is used from the moment the child can spread its legs, until it is about two years old.

2. Bend over forwards. Lay the child on your back with its legs apart. Lay the cloth over the child. The top edge of the cloth is at the level of the child's neck.

1. Take a cloth measuring about 90cm by 1.20m (3 by 4 feet).

3. Tuck the legs in.

4. Take the two upper corners of the cloth. Twist them around each other twice firmly.

6. Take the two lower corners of the cloth. Do the same with these as with the other corners. Stand up straight.

5. Tuck the twisted ends in: roll the cloth outwards.

On the back in a carry-bag

When European bath towels were first imported into Zimbabwe, people also started using them as carrying cloths. However, the towels were shorter than the original African cloths, and the knot often came loose. The government commissioned the design of a cheap and safe bag, which can be bought all over the country. For decoration, women often wrap a colourful cloth around the canvas. It is used from the moment the child can spread its legs until it is three or four years old.

You can make the bag yourself using the pattern. Use a sturdy fabric, preferably canvas.

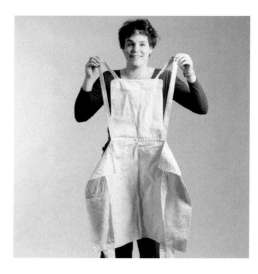

1. Take the sling.

2. Put it on like a rucksack. Tie the straps around your stomach.

3. Bend over forwards. Lay the child on your back with its legs apart.

5. Tie them to the straps around your stomach.

4. Bring the straps that are hanging loose forwards over your shoulders.

Pattern (measurements in cm)

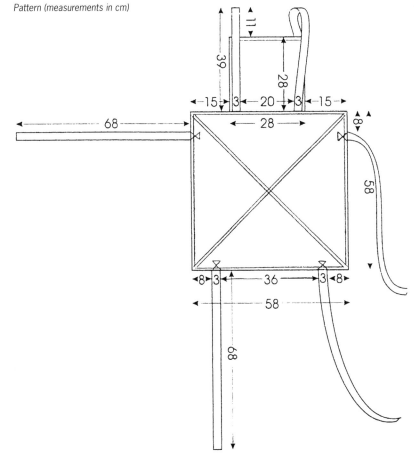

Bibliography

Reference Material, General

Barr, R.G., Bakeman, R., Konner, M. et al, 'Crying in Kung infants: a test of the cultural specificity hypothesis'. *Developmental Medicine and Child Neurology* 33 (1991) pp. 601-10.

Barr, R.G., McMullan, S.J., Spiess, H. et al, 'Carrying as colic 'therapy': a randomized controlled trial'. *Pediactrics* 87 (1991) pp. 623-30.

Billmer, H.J.T., *De evolutie van de mens*. The Hague, Servire, 1946.

Bloch, A., 'The Kurdistan cradle story: a modern analysis of this centuries-old infant swaddling practice'. *Clinical Pediatrics*, October 1966.

Bolk, L., *Hersenen en cultuur*. Amsterdam, Scheltema en Holkema, 1918.

Bowlby, J., *Attachment and Loss*. Vol.1 *Attachment*. London, 1982.

Catlin, G., *Drawings of the North American Indians*. New York, 1984.

Chisholm, J.S., Richards, M., 'Swaddling, cradleboards and the development of children'. *Early Human Development* 1978, no. 2.

Cocks, L., 'Van placenta tot placebo'. *Medische Antropologie* 1 (1989) no. 1.

Cohen, D., *De Cirkel van het leven*. Utrecht/Antwerpen, 1992.

Cohn, A.R., Leach, L.A., *Generations. A Universal Family Album*. New York, Pantheon Books, 1987.

Cultural Palace of Nationalities (ed.), *Clothing and Ornaments of China's Miao People*. Beijing, 1985.

Denham, W.W., 'Infant transport among the Alyawara tribe, Central Australia'. *Oceania* XLIV (1974) no. 4.

Disselhoff, H.D., 'Nordamerikanische Kinderwiegen im Berliner Museum für Völkerkunde'. *Baessler-Archiv* Band XX. Berlin, 1937.

Dubin, L. Sherr, *The history of beads*. London, Thames and Hudson, 1987.

Duncan, K.C., Carney, E., *A special gift: the Kutchin beadwork tradition*. Seattle etc., University of Washington Press, 1988.

Fisher, A., *Africa adorned*. London etc., 1985.

Garrett, V.M., *The children of the Gods*. Hongkong, 1990.

Geest, S. van der, 'Medicijn, metafoor en metonymia'. *Medische Antropologie* 2 (1990) no. 1.

Gennep, A. van, *Rites de Passage*. Paris, 1909.

Gould, S.J., 'Human babies as embryos'. in: Cohn, A.R. and L.A. Leach (eds.), *Generations. A universal family album*. New York, 1987.

Hinde, R.A., *Biological bases of human social behaviour*. New York, McGraw-Hill, 1974.

Hodge, F.W., *Handbook of American Indians*. Vol. I. New York, 1960.

Hunziker, U.A., Barr, R.G., 'Increased carrying reduces infant crying: a randomized controlled trial'. *Pediactrics* 77 (1986) no. 5, pp. 641-8.

Jackson, J.W., *Shells as evidence of the migration of early culture*. London, 1917.

Kenntner, G., *Gebräuche und Leistungsfähigkeit des Menschen im Tragen von Lasten*. Den Haag, 1973.

Kitzinger, S., *Women as Mothers*. New York, 1979.

Knuf, A., Knuf, J., *Amulette und Talismane: Symbole des Magischen Alltags*. Köln, Dumont, 1984.

Kroeber, A.L., *The Arapaho*. Washington, 1979.

La Fontaine, J.S., *Initiation*. London, 1984.

Leeuw, R. de, Bakker, L., *Te vroeg geboren*. Ede, Zomer en Keuning, 1989.

Leeuw, R. de, 'De kangoeroemethode'. *Ned. Tijdschr. Geneesk.* 131 (1987) pp. 1484-7.

Leeuw, R. de, Colin, E.M., Dunnebier, E.A. et al, 'Physiological effects of kangaroo care in very small preterm infants'. *Biol Neonate* 59 (1991) pp. 149-55.

Levi Strauss, C., *Het wilde denken*. Amsterdam, Meulenhoff, 1976.

Man, *A record of anthropological science* no. 71, 1942.

Martínez Gómez, H. y J.R. Aguilar (eds.), *Programa Madre Canguro. Primer Encuentro Internacional*. Bogotá (Colombia), Unicef, 1990.

Mason, O.T., *Cradles of the American Aborigines*. From the Report of the National Museum Washington, 1889.

Mellaart, J., *The Goddess from Anatolia*. London, Thames and Hudson, 1990.

Minor, M., Minor, N., *The American Indian craft book*. Nebraska, [s.a.].

Morris, W.F., *A millennium of weaving in Chiapas*. Chiapas, Mexico, 1986.

Murdock, G.P., *Atlas of world cultures*. Pittsburgh, University of Pittsburgh Press, 1981.

Naaktgeboren, C., *Het aangenomen kind*. Deventer, 1988.

Naaktgeboren, C., *Ouders en kinderen. Vruchtbaarheid, zwangerschap en geboorte in verschillende culturen*. Deventer, 1988.

Pastoureau, M., *L'Etoffe du diable*. Paris, Seuil, 1991.

Paul, S., 'Ethnologische und Biologische Aspekte. Schwangerschaft, Geburt und Stillzeit in ethnologischer Sicht'. In: Schindler, S., *Geburt, Eintritt in eine neue Welt*. Göttingen, 1982.

Pflug, W., 'Die Kinderwiege, ihre Formen and ihre Verbreitung'. *Archiv für Anthropologie* N.F. Band XIX, 1923.

Ploss, H., *Das kleine Kind vom Tragbett Bis Zum Ersten Schritt*. Berlin, 1881.

Ploss, H., *Das Kind: in Brauch und Sitte der Völker*. Leipzig, 1884.

Pokrowski, E., *Matériaux pour servir à l'étude de l'éducation physique chez les différents peuples de l'empire Russe*. Moscow, 1989.

Sears, W., 'Wearing your baby'. *Mothering*, winter 1989.

Spier, F., 'Indiaanse genezing; macht en afhankelijkheid in de Peruaanse Andes: een case study'. *Medische Antropologie* 1 (1989) no. 1.

Spitz, R.A., 'Institutionalized infants. Hospitalism: an inquiry into the genesis of psychiatric conditions in early childhood'. in: Stone, L., H. Smith. L. Murphy (eds.), *The competent infant*. New York, Basic Books, 1973.

Stenbak, E., 'Care of children in hospital'. In: *Kind en Ziekenhuis*, maart 1993.

Veldhuisen-Djajasoebrata, A., *Bloemen van het heelal. De kleurrijke wereld van het textiel op Java*. Amsterdam, Sijthoff, 1984.

Walraven J., *Kleur*. Ede, Zomer en Keuning, 1981.

Whitelaw, A., 'Kangaroo baby care: just a nice experience or an important advance for preterm infants?' *Pediatrics* 85 (1990) pp. 604-5.

Whitelaw, A., Sleath, K., 'Myth of the marsupial mother: home care of very low birth-weight babies in Bogotá, Colombia'. *Lancet* 1 (1985) pp. 1206-9.

Whiting, J.W.M., 'Effects of climate on certain cultural practices'. In: Goudenough, W.H. (ed.), *Explorations in cultural anthropology*. New York, 1964.

Whittier, H.L., *Social organization and symbols of social differentiation: and ethnographic study of the Kenyah Dayak of East Kalimantan*. Ann Arbor, 1973.

Africa

Alberti, L., *Ludwig Alberti's account of the tribal life and customs of the Xhosa in 1807*. Transl. from the orig. manuscript in German by W. Febr. Cape Town, Balkema, 1968.

Anderson, S. and Staugard, F., *Traditional midwives: traditional medicine in Botswana*. Gaberone, Ipelegeng Publishers, 1986.

Aronson, L., 'The language of West African textiles'. *African Arts XXV*, no. 3, pp. 36-40. Los Angeles, 1962.

Aronson, L., 'Ljebu Yoruba Aso Olona: a contextual and historical overview'. *African Arts XXV*, no. 3, pp. 52-63. Los Angeles, 1962.

Broster, J., *Amagoirha: religion, magic and medicine in Transkei*. Goodwood, Via Africa, 1982.

Bryant, A.T., *Olden times in Zululand and Natal*. London, Longmans, 1929.

Bubolz Eicher, J., *Nigerian handcrafted textiles*. Lagos, 1976.

Bullock, C., *The Mashona*. Cape Town, Juta, 1927.

Chalmers, B., *African birth: childbirth in cultural transition*. Berev Publications, 1990.

Christaller, J.G., *A dictionary of the Asante and Fante language called Tshi (Twi)*. Basel, 1933.

Cole, H.M. and Ross, D.H., *The arts of Ghana*. Los Angeles, 1977.

Crownover, D., *The art of goldweights: words, form, meaning*. Philadelphia, Anko Foundation etc., 1977.

Dapper, O., *Umbständliche und eigenliche Beschreibung von Africa, und denen darzu gehörigen Königreichen und Landschaften*. Meurs, 1670.

Dasen, P., Inhelder, B., Lavallee, M. et al, *Naissance de l'intelligence chez les Baoulé de Cote D'Ivoire*. Bern etc., Hans Huber, 1978

De Lestrange, M.Th. et Gessain, M., *Collections Bassari du Musée de l'Homme*. Paris, 1976.

Desieux, C. et P., Bonnet, D., *Africaines*. L'Harmattan, 1983.

Erny, P., *Les Premiers pas dans la vie de l'enfant d'Afrique noire*. L'Harmattan, 1988.

Falade, S., *Le développement psychomoteur du jeune Africain originaire du Sénégal au cours de la première année*. Paris, Foulon 1955.

Graffenried, Ch. von, *Akan Goldgewichte/Goldweights*. Bern 1990.

Hammond-Tooke, D., Nettleton, A., *Ten years of collecting 1979-1989*. Johannesburg, University of Witwatersrand 1989

Hunter, M., *Reaction to conquest*. London, Oxford University Press, 1969.

Krige, E. Jensen, 'Individual development'. In: Schapera (ed.) *The Bantu speaking tribes of South Africa*. Cape Town, Maskew Miller, 1937.

Krige, E. Jensen, *The social system of the Zulus*. Pietermantzburg (South Africa), Shuter & Shuter, 1965.

Lallemand, S., *Un petit sujet*. J.S.A. 51 (sous la direction de G. Le Moal). 1981.

Lamb, V. and Holmes, J., *Nigerian weaving*. Roxford, 1980.

Laydevant, F., *The Basutu*. Lesotho, St. Michael's Mission, 1952.

Lestrade, G.P., 'Domestic and communal life'. In: Schapera, I. (ed.), *The Bantu speaking tribes of South Africa*. Cape Town, 1937.

McLeod, M., *Ashanti goldweights*. London, British Museum Publications, 1976.

Menzel, B., *Goldgewichte aus Ghana*. Berlin, Museum für Völkerkunde, 1968.

Meyerowitz, E.L.R., *The Akan of Ghana: their ancient beliefs*. London, 1958.

Ortigues, M.C. et E., *Oedipe Africain*. Plon, 1966.

Paul, S., 'Afrikanische Puppen'. *Baessler-archiv* N.F. 6 (1970).

Pauw, B.A., *The second generation: Xhosa in town*. Cape Town, Oxford University Press, 1969.

Picton, J., Mack, J., *African textiles*. London, 1979.

Rabain, J., *L'enfant du lignage*. Payot, 1979.

Rattray, R.S., *Ashanti*. Oxford, 1923.

Rattray, R.S., *Religion and art in Ashanti*. London, 1959.

Rijn, G. van (ed.), *Goldweights/Goudgewichten*. Amsterdam, 1979.

Schapera, I. (ed.), *The Bantu speaking people of South Africa*. Cape Town, Maskew Miller, 1937.

Schapera, I., *The early Cape Hottentots, described in the writings of Olfert Dapper (1668)*. Cape Town, Van Riebeek Society, 1933.

Schapera, I., *Married life in an African tribe*. Harmondsworth, Pelican Books, 1971.

Shaw, E.M., Warmelo, N.J. van, 'The material culture of the Cape Nguni'. *Annals of the South African Museum 58* (1972).

Textiellexicon, *verklarend weeftechnisch woordenboek*. Amsterdam, 1991.

Traore, D., *Médecine et magies Africaines*. PUF, 1965.

Tremearne, A.J.N., *Hausa superstitions and customs: an introduction to the folklore and the folk*. London, 1970.

Tyrrell, B., *African heritage*. Johannesburg, Macmillan, 1986.

Tyrrell, B., *Tribal people of Southern Africa*. Cape Town, Gothic Printing, 1968.

Vedder, H., *The native tribes of South West Africa*. Cape Town, Cape Times Ltd., 1928.

Witte. H., *Earth and ancestors: Ogboni iconography*. Amsterdam

Zeller. R., 'Die Goldgewichte von Asante (Westafrika)'. *Baessler-Archiv* 3 (1912)

Europe

Brown. Chr., *Scenes of everyday life. Dutch genre painting of the fifteenth century*. Amsterdam, 1984.

Cunnington, Ph. and A. Buck, *Children's costume in England from the fourteenth to the end of the nineteenth century*. London, 1965.

Franck van Berkhey, Johannes Le, *Natuurlyke historie van Holland*. Amsterdam 1769-1779, deel 3.

Frans Hals Museum, *Portretten van echt en trouw. Huwelijk en Gezin in de Nederlandse kunst van de zeventiende eeuw*. Zwolle, 1986

Hamelsveld, Y. van, *De zedelijke toestand der Nederlandsche natie*. Amsterdam, 1791, p.174 et seq.

Haneveld, G.T., 'De valhoedt'. *Spiegel historiael* 8 (1973) p.462 et seq.

Haskell, A. and M. Lewis, *Infantilia. The archeology of nursery*. London, 1971.

Kloek, W.Th., *Alleen kijken naar meisjes of jongetjes*. Rijksmuseum Amsterdam, Dec. 1977-Mar. 1978.

Muller, S.D., *Charity in the Dutch Republic*. Michigan, 1985.

Reinold, L.K., *The representation of the beggar as rogue in Dutch seventeenth-century art*. Michigan, 1983.

Schama, S., *Overvloed en onbehagen. De Nederlandse cultuur in de Gouden Eeuw.* Amsterdam, 1987.

Schilstra, W.N., *Vrouwenarbeid in landbouw en industrie in Nederland in de tweede helft der negentiende eeuw.* Reprint. Nijmegen, 1976.

Vandebroeck, P., *Over wilden en narren, boeren en bedelaars. Beeld van de andere, vertoog over het zelf.* Antwerpen, 1987.

Vogler, K., *Die Ikonographie der Flucht nach Aegypten.* Heidelberg, 1930.

Warner, G. (ed.), *Queen Mary's psalter. Miniatures and drawings by an English artist of the 14th century.* London, 1912.

Warner, M., *Alone of all her sex. The myth and the cult of the Virgin Mary.* London, 1976.

America

Brommer, B. (ed.), *3000 jaar weven in de Andes. Textiel uit Peru en Bolivia.* Helmond, Gemeente Museum Helmond, 1988.

Chrisholm, J.S., *Navajo infancy: an ethnological study of child development.* Chicago, Aldine, 1983.

Cody, B.P., 'California Indian baby cradles'. *Masterkey* 14 (1940) pp. 89-96.

D'Harcourt, R., *Textiles of ancient Peru and their techniques.* Seattle, University of Washington Press, 1962.

De Laguna, F., *Under Mount St. Elias, the history and culture of the Yakutat Tlingit.* Washington DC, 1972. (Smithsonian Institution Contributions to Anthropology 7)

Dellinger, S.C., 'Baby cradles of the Ozark Bluff Dwellers'. *American antiquity* 1 (1936) pp. 197-214.

Dennis, W., *The Hopi child.* Repr. New York, Arno Press, 1972.

Dennis, W. and M.G. Dennis, 'Cradles and cradling practices of the Pueblo Indians'. *American Anthropologist* 42 (1940) pp. 107-15.

Driver, H.A., *Indians of North America.* Second rev. ed. Chicago, University of Chicago Press, 1969.

Emery, I., *The primary structures of fabric.* Washington DC, The Textile Museum, 1980.

Erikson, E.H., 'Observations on Sioux education'. *Journal of psychology* 7 (1939) pp. 101-56.

Erikson, E.H., *Childhood and society.* New York, Norton, 1950

Farrabee, W. Curtis, *Indian cradles. University of Pennsylvania Museum Journal* 11 (1920) pp. 183-211

Flores Ochoa, J.F., *'El Cuzco': resistencia y continuidad.* Cusco Centro de Estudios Andinos, 1980.

Freedman, J.G., *Human infancy: an evolutionary perspective.* Hillsdale, Lawrence Erlbaum, 1974.

Garbarino, M.S., *Big cypress: a changing Seminole community.* New York, Holt, Rinehart and Winston, 1972.

Gilbert, W.H., *The Eastern Cherokees.* Washington DC Bureau for American Anthropology, 1943. (Bulletin 133).

Gilmore, R., 'The Northern Arapaho cradle'. *American Indian Art Magazine* 16 (1990) no. 1. pp. 64-71.

Hilger, Sister I.M., *Arapaho child life and its cultural background.* Washington DC, Bureau of American Ethnology, 1952 (Bulletin 148)

Holm, B., *Spirit and ancestor: a century of Northwest Coast Indian art at the Burke Museum.* Seattle, University of Washington Press, 1987.

Howard, J.H. and Lena, W., *Oklahoma Seminoles: medicines, magic and religion.* Norman, University of Oklahoma Press, 1984.

Hungry Wolf, B., *The ways of my grandmothers.* New York, Quill, 1982.

Jones, R.L. and Whitmore-Ostlund, C., 'Cradles of life'. *American Indian Art Magazine* 5 (1980) no. 4, pp. 36-41.

Kandt, Vera B., *Peruaanse textielen.* Rotterdam, Museum voor Volkenkunde, 1979.

Kenntner, G., *Gebräuche und Leistungsfähigkeit des Menschen im Tragen von Lasten.* The Hague, 1973.

Latta, F.F., *Handbook of Yokuts Indians.* Bakersfield, California Kern County Museum, 1949.

Leighton, D. and Kluckhohn, C., *Children of the people: the Navaho individual and his development.* Cambridge, Harvard University Press, 1947.

Lenz, M.J., *The stuff of dreams. Native American dolls.* New York, Museum of the American Indian, 1986.

Lessard, R., 'Lakota cradles'. *American Indian Art Magazine* 16 (1990) no. 1, pp. 44-53.

Lipton, E., Steinschneider, A. and Richmond, J., 'Swaddling. a child care practice'. *Pediatrics* 35 (1965) pp. 519-67.

Loeb, E.M., *Pomo folkways.* Berkeley, University of California Press, 1926.

Mason, O.T., 'Cradles of the American aborigines'. In: *annual report of the united states national museum* 1887-1889.

Mead, M., 'The swaddling hypothesis: its reception'. *American Anthropologist* 56 (1954) no. 3, pp. 395-409.

Niethammer, C., *Daughters of the earth: the lives and legends of American Indian women.* New York, MacMillan, 1977.

Opler, M.E., *Childhood and youth in Vicarilla Apache society.* New York, Southwest Museum, 1946.

Pettitt, G.A., *Primitive education in North America*. Berkeley, University of California Press, 1946.

Prochaska, Rita, *Taquile: Tejiendo un mondo màgico. Weaves of a magic world*. Lima, Arius, 1988.

Rowe, A. Pollard, *Warp-patterned weaves of the Andes*. Washington DC, The Textile Museum, 1977.

Schneider, M.J., 'Kiowa and Comanche baby carriers'. *Plains Anthropologist* 28 (1983) pp. 305-14.

Silvermann-Proust, G.P., 'Cuatro motivos Inti de Q'ero'. *Boletin de Lima* 43 (1986) pp. 61-76.

Smithson, C.L., *The Havasupai woman*. Salt Lake City, University of Utah Press, 1959.

Walters, A.L., *The spirit of native America: beauty and mysticism in American Indian art*. San Francisco, 1989.

Zorn, E., 'Un anáisis de los tejidos en los atados rituales de los pastores'. REVISTA ANDINA 5 (1987) no. 2, pp. 489-526.

Asia

Andreev, M.S., *De Tadzjieken van het Choef-dal. (Werken van het Historisch, Archeologisch en Etnografisch Instituut van de Tadzjiekse ssr, deel 7)*. [M.S. Andreev, *Tadziki doliny Chuf. (Trudy Instituta istorii, archeologii i etnografii an Tadzikskoj SSR, t. 7)*]. Stalinabad, 1953.

Beukers en Beukers, *Handwerken zonder grenzen* no. 1 en 3, 1987.

Chamidzianova, M.A., 'Patterns from pieces of fabric'. *The Tajiks of Karatecin and Darvaz*. [M.A. Chamidzianova, 'Uzornye izdelija iz kusockov materii'. *Tadziki Karategina i Darvaza*. pp. 225-57 Dushanbe, 1970.

Chamidzianova, M., 'Enkele opvattingen van de Tadzjieken over slangen'. *Studies of the Institute for History, Archeology and Ethnography of the Tajiki SSR*, part CXX. [M. Chamidzianova, 'Nekotorye predstavienija tadzikov, svjazannye so zmeej'. *Trudy Instituta istorii, archeologii i etnografii an Tadzikskoj SSR, t. CXX*, pp. 215-23]. Stalinabad, 1960.

Elshout, J.M., *Over de geneeskunde der Kenja-Dajak in verband met hunnen godsdienst*. Amsterdam, Muller, 1923.

Frezer, D., *De geode twijg*. [D. Frezer, *Zolotaja vetv*, p.50]. Moscow/Leningrad, 1931.

Garret V.M., *Dress and symbolism in China*.

Geirnaert, D.C. and Heringa, R., *The Aedta batik collection*. Paris, Association pour l'Etude et la Documentation des Textiles d'Asie, 1989.

Heringa, R., 'Kain Tuban. Een oude Javaanse indigo-traditie'. In: Loan Oei (red.), *Indigo. Leven in een kleur*, pp. 115-20. Amsterdam, Stichting Indigo, 1985.

Heringa, R., 'Textiel en wereldbeeld in Tuban'. In: Schefold, R. et al, *Indonesia apa kabarp?*, pp. 55-61. Meppel, Edu'Actief, 1988.

Heringa, R., 'Dye-process and life-sequence. The coloring of textiles in an East Javanese village'. In: Gittinger, M. (ed.), *To speak with cloth*, pp. 107-39. Los Angeles, Museum of Cultural History, University of California Press, 1989.

Heringa, R., Unpublished field notes. 1989-90.

Hose, Ch. and McDougall, W., *The pagan tribes of Borneo*. 2 Vols. Reprint. London, Frank Cass, 1966 (1912).

Jansz, P., *Practisch Javaansch-Nederlandsch woordenboek*. Tweede druk. Den Haag, Van Dorp, 1913.

Litvinskij, B.A., 'De spiegel in het geloof van de oude Ferganen'. *Sovjet etnografie*. [B.A. Litvinskij, 'Zerkalo v verovaniach drevnich Fergancev'. *Sovetskaja etnografia*] no. 3, 1964, pp. 97-104.

Lumboltz, C., *Through Central Borneo*. New York, Charles Scribner, 1920.

Nieuwenhuis, A.W., *Quer durch Borneo*. 2 Vols. Leiden, E.J. Brill, 1904.

Roth, H. Ling, *The natives of Sarawak and British North Borneo*. 2 Vols. London, Truslove and Hanson, 1896.

Rouffaer, G.P. and H.H. Juynboll, *De batikkunst in Nederlandsch Indië en hare geschiedenis*. Utrecht, Rijks Ethnologisch Museum, 1914.

Snesarev, G.P., *Relicten van voor-islamitische geloven en rituelen bij de Chorezm-Oezbeken*. [G.P. Snesarev, *Relikty domusul manskich verovanij i obrjadov u Uzbekov Chorezma*, p.79]. Moscow, 1968.

Sojunova, A., 'De wieg in ritueel en religie van de Toerkmenen'. *Materiaal over de historische etnografie van de Toerkmenen*. [A. Sojunova, 'Kolybel v obrjadach i verovani-jach Turkmen'. *Materialy po istoriceskoj etnografii Turkmen*, pp. 71-83]. Ashchabad, 1987.

Suchareva, O.A., 'Over de resten van de wilgencultus bij de Tadzjieken'. *Het verleden van Centraal-Azië*. [O.A. Suchareva, 'O perezitkach kul'ta ivy u tadzikov'. *Prosloe Srednej Azii*, pp. 251-60]. Dushanbe, 1987.

St. John, Sir Spenser, *Life in the forests of the Far East*. 2 Vols. London, Elder Smith, 1862.

Tillema, H.F., *Apokajan: een filmreis naar en door Centraal-Borneo*. Amsterdam, Van Munster, 1938.

Whittier, H.L., *Social organization and symbols of social differentiation: an ethnographic study of the Kenyah Dayak of East Kalimantan (Borneo)*. Ann Arbor, Michigan State University, Dept. of Anthropology, 1973. (Thesis)

Whittier, P.R., *Systems of appellation among the Kenyah Dayak of Borneo*. Ann Arbor, Michigan State University, Dept. of Anthropology, 1981. (Thesis)

Zarubin, 1.1., 'De geboorte van een Sjoeknan kind en zijn eerste stappen'. Anthology: *Voor V.V. Bartoljd, Toerkestanse vrienden, leerlingen en bewonderaars*. [I.I. Zarubin, 'Rozdenie sugnanskogo rebenka i ego pervye Sagi'. *Bartol'du Turkestanskie druz'ja, uceniki i pocitateli*, pp. 361-73]. Tashkent, 1927.

Zheng Lan, *Travels through Xishuangbanna*.

Zoetmulder, P.J. and S.O. Robson, *Old-Javanese-English dictionary*. 2 Vols. The Hague, Martinus Nijhoff, 1982.

Oceania

Beier, U. and A. Maori Kiki, *Hohao: the uneasy survival of an art form in the Papuan Gulf*. London etc., Nelson, 1970.

Bodrogi, T., *Art in North-East New Guinea*. Budapest, Publishing House of the Hungarian Academy of Sciences, 1961.

Bowden, R., *Yena: art and ceremony in a Sepik society*. Oxford, Pitt Rivers Museum etc., 1983. (Monograph 3).

Chowning, A., 'Child rearing and socialization'. In: Ryan, P. (ed.), *Encyclopaedia of Papua and New Guinea II*, pp. 156-64. Carlton (Victoria), Melbourne University Press etc., 1972.

Craig, B., *Art and decoration of Central New Guinea*. Aylesbury, Shire Publications, 1988.

Eoe, Soroi M., The Elema. Bathurst, Robert Brown and Associates, 1984. (People of Papua New Guinea, ed. A.L. Crawford).

Gell, A., *Metamorphosis of the Cassowaries: Umeda society, language and ritual*. London etc., Athlone Press etc., 1975.

Harding, Thomas G., *Voyagers of the Vitiaz Strait: a study of a New Guinea trade system*. Seattle etc., University of Washington Press, 1967.

Harrison, S., 'Concepts of the person in Avatip religious thought'. In: Lutkehaus, N. et al (eds.), *Sepik heritage: tradition and change in Papua New Guinea*, pp. 351-63. Durham (North Carolina), Carolina Academic Press, 1990.

Hauser-Schäublin, *Frauen in Kararau: zur Rolle der Frau bei den Iatmul am Mittelsepik, Papua New Guinea*. Basel, Ethnologisches Seminar der Universität und Museum für Völkerkunde, 1977.

Hauser-Schäublin, *Leben in Linie, Muster und Farbe: Einführung in die Betrachtung aussereuropäischer Kunst am Beispiel der Abelam, Papua-Neuguinea*. Basel etc., Birkhäuser Verlag, 1989.

Heider, K.G., *The Dugum Dani: a Papuan culture in the highlands of West New Guinea*. Chicago, Aldine Publishing Company, 1970.

Herdt, G.H. (ed.), *Rituals of manhood: male initiation in Papua New Guinea*. (Introduction by R.M. Keesing). Berkeley etc., University of California Press, 1982.

Hinderling, P., 'Stoffbildendes Schnurverschlingen'. *Baesslerarchiv* N.F. 32 (1959) no. 7, pp. 1-79.

Hylkema, S., *Mannen in het draagnet: mens- en wereldbeeld van de Nalum (Sterrengebergte)*. The Hague, Martinus Nijhoff, 1974.

Kaufmann, Christian, *Kwoma (Neuguinea, Sepik): herstellen einer Tragtasche in Maschenstofftechnik / Kwoma (New Guinea, Sepik: manufacture of a carrying bag in knotless netting technique)*. Göttingen: Institut für den wissenschaftlichen Film, 1980.

Kaufmann, Chr., 'Maschenstoffe und ihre gesellschaftliche Funktion am Beispiel der Kwoma von Papua-Neuguinea'. *Tribus* 35 (1986) pp. 127-75.

Koch, G., *Kultur der Abelam: die Berliner 'Maprik'-Sammlung*. Berlin, Museum für Völkerkunde, 1968.

Kocher Schmid, C., *Of people and plants: a botanical ethnography of Nokopo village, Madang and Morobe provinces, Papua New Guinea*. Basel, Ethnologisches Seminar der Universität und Museum für Völkerkunde, 1991.

Kooijman, S., 'Material aspects of the Star Mountains culture: scientific results of the Netherlands New Guinea expedition 1959'. *Nova Guinea, N.S. 10, Anthropology 2* (1962) pp. 15-44, plates 1-XX, figs. 1-71. Leiden, E.J. Brill.

MacKenzie, M.A., 'The Telefol string bag: a cultural object with androgynous forms'. In: Craig B. and D. Hyndman (eds.), *Children of Afek: tradition and change among the Mountain-Ok of Central New Guinea*, pp. 88-108. Sydney, Sydney University, 1990.

MacKenzie, M.A., *Androgynous objects: string bags and gender in Central New Guinea*. Chur, Harwood Academic Publishers, 1991.

Mangal, P. and D. Smidt, *The Kominimung*. Revised ed. Boroko, National Cultural Council etc., 1984. (People of Papua New Guinea, ed. A.L. Crawford).

Powell, J.M., 'Ethnobotany'. In: Paijmans, K. (ed.), *New

Guinea Vegetation, pp. 106-83. Canberra, Commonwealth Scientific and Industrial Research Organization etc., 1976.

Roux, C.C.F.M. Le. *De Bergpapoea's van Nieuw-Guinea en hun woongebied*. 3 volumes. Leiden, E.J. Brill, 1948-50.

Schieffelin, E.L., *The sorrow of the lonely and the burning of the dancers*. New York, St. Martin's Press, 1976.

Schuster, G., *Begleitpublikation zum Film E 1373: Aibom Neuguinea, Mittlerer Sepik): Gewinnen und Färben von Rindenbaststreifen*. Göttingen, Institut für den Wissenschaftlichen Film, 1981.

Schuster, G., 'Netztaschen der Zentral-Iatmul im Museum für Völkerkunde Basel'. In: Engelbrecht, B. und B. Gardi (eds.), *Man does not go naked: Textilien und Handwerk aus afrikanischen und anderen Ländern*, pp. 335-89. Basel, Ethnologisches Seminar der Universität und Museum für Völkerkunde, 1989.

Schwimmer, E., *Exchange in the social structure of the Orokaiva: traditional and emergent ideologies in the Northern district of Papua*. London, Hurst & Company, 1973.

Seiler-Baldinger, A., *Systematik der Textilen Techniken*. Basel, Ethnologisches Seminar der Universität und Museum für Völkerkunde, 1991.

Sillitoe, P., *Made in Niugini: technology in the Highlands of Papua New Guinea*. London, British Museum Publications etc., 1988.

Smidt, Dirk, 'Geboorte op Nieuw-Guinea'. In: Dongen, P.L.F. van, Th.J.J. Levenaar en K. Vos (eds.), *De jaargetijden van de mens*, pp. 17-24. Leiden, Rijksmuseum voor Volkenkunde, 1987.

Smidt, Dirk, 'Initiatie-rituelen op Nieuw-Guinea en Nieuw-Brittannië'. In: P.L.F. van Dongen et al (eds.), *De jaargetijden van de mens*, pp. 26-36. Leiden, Rijksmuseum voor Volkenkunde. 1987.

Smidt, Dirk, Unpublished field notes, Abelam Sepik-region, East Sepik Province, Papua New Guinea 1987

Smidt, Dirk. Unpublished field notes, Kominimung and Rao, Central Ramu region, Madang Province Papua New Guinea 1976 -1979.

Strathern, A. and M. *Self-decoration in Mount Hagen*. London, Gerald Duckworth. 1971 (Art and Society Series, ed. Peter J. Ucko)

Weiss, F., *Kinder schildern ihren Alltag. Die Stellung des Kindes im ökonomischen System einer Dorfgemeinschaft in Papua New Guinea (Palimbei, Iatmul, Mittelsepik*. Basel Ethnologisches Seminar der Universität und Museum für Völkerkunde, 1981.

Around the Arctic circle

Bernatzik, H.A., *Lapland*. London, 1938. (German original, 1935).

Bye, Lilian, *'Finner i Finnmark*. Oslo, 1939.

Chomic, L.V., 'De draagwieg bij Siberische volkeren (wat betreft typologie)'. Anthology: *Materiele en geestelijke cultuur van de Siberische volkeren*. [L.V. Chomic, 'Kolybel' u narodov Sibiti (k voprosu o tipologii'). Sb. *Maè Material'naja i duchovnaja kul'tura narodov Sibiri*, pp. 24-49]. Leningrad, 1988.

Chomic, L.V., 'De draagwieg als historische bron bij Oegrischsamodijsische volkeren'. Anthology: *Hedendaagse kennis over Fins-Oegrische volkeren. Onderzoek en vraagstelling*. [L.V. Chomic, 'Kolybel' u ugro-samodijskich narodov kak istoriceskij istocik'. Sb. *Sobremennoe Finno-ugrovedenie. Opyt i problemy*, pp. 77-80]. Leningrad, 1990.

Demant Hatt, E., *Med Lapparne i Höjfjeldet*. Copenhagen, 1913.

Driscoll, B., Swinton, G., *The Inuit Amautik. Exhibition catalogue*. Winnipeg, Winnipeg Art Gallery, 1980.

Dupaigne, B., Robbe, B., *Chez les Eskimo (Côte Est du Groenland)*. Musée de l'Homme. Paris, Editions du Muséum National d'Histoire Naturelle, 1989.

Elgström, Ossian, *Karesuandolapparna, etnografiska skisser från Kongämä och Lainiovuoma 1916-1919*. Stockholm, 1922.

Fedorova, E.G., 'Het kind in het traditionele Mansen gezin'. Anthology: *De traditionele opvoeding van kinderen bij Siberische volkeren....* [E.G. Fedorova, 'Rebenok v tradicionnoj mansijskoj sem'e'. Sb. *Tradicionnoe vospitanie detej u narodov Sibiri...*], pp. 80-2.

Fjellström, Phebe, *Lapskt Silver I. Studier över en föremålsgrupp och dess ställning inom lapskt kulturliv*. Uppsala, 1962.

Friis, Jens A., *Lajla. Een liefde in Lapland*. Amsterdam, s.a.

Getz, B., 'Medfødt holteleddsluksasjon hos lapper'. *Tidsskrift for Den norske lægeforening* 76 (1956) pp. 812-6.

Grundström, Harald, 'Tro och övertro bland lapparna'. *Svenska Landsmål och svenskt Folkliv* 65 (1942) pp. 5-30.

Guttorm, Gunvor, *Gietkka*. Kautokeino, 1991.

Hogguér, Freih. Daniel von. *Vildmarksliv i Lappland för hundra År sedan*. Översatt och försedd med inledning av Harry Blomberg. Stockholm, 1928. (German original 1841).

Johansson, C., 'Något om lapsk spädbarnsvård i äldre tider'. *Svenska Landsmål och svenskt Folkliv* 89 (1966) pp. 62-73.

Kloster, J., 'The distribution and frequency of rickets in one of the fishery districts of Finnmark and relation of the diet to the disorder'. *Acta Paediatrica* 12, suppl. 3. Uppsala, 1931.

Kulemzin, V.M., *De mens en de natuur in het geloof van de Chanten.* [V.M. Kulemzin, *Celovek i priroda v verovanijach chantov*, pp. 106-7]. Tomsk, 1984.

Nooter, G., 'Leadership and headship. Changing authority patterns in an East-Greenland hunting community'. In: *Mededelingen van het rijksmuseum voor volkenkunde* 20, pp. 1-117. Leiden, 1976.

Pirak, Anta, *En Nomad och hans Liv*, upptecknat och översatt av H.Grundström. Uppsala, 1933.

Rheen, Samuele, 'En kortt Relation om Lapparnes Lefwarne och Sedher, wijdskiepellsser, sampt i många Stycken Grofwe wildfarellsser'. *Bidrag till Kännedom om de svenska Landsmålen ock svenskt Folkliv* XVII, 1. Uppsala, 1897.

Robbe, B., 'Le traitement des peaux de phoque chez les Ammassalimiut observé en 1972 dans le village de Tîlegilaq'. *Objets et mondes. La revue du Musée de l'Homme* 15 (1975) no. 2, pp. 199-208.

Robbe, B., 'Tradition et changement du rôle et des activités des femmes de chasseurs dans un village de la *côte Est du Groenland* '. *Actes du 42ème congres international des Américanistes*. Paris, 2-9 septembre 1976, no. 5, pp. 83-9.

Robbe, B., 'Poupées Inuit'. In: Battesti, T., *Poupée jouet, poupée reflet.* Musée de l'Homme. Paris, Muséum National d'Histoire Naturelle, 1983. Robbe, B., 'Rôles et marges dans la division sexuelle des tâches dans une société de chasseurs Inuit'. In: *Sexe et genre. Collection "Le Sociologue"*. Paris, Presses Universitaires de France, 1993.

Robbe, P., *Le chasseur Arctique et son milieu: stratégies individuelles et collectives des Inuit d'Ammasalik.* Paris, Muséum National d'Histoire Naturelle, 1993. (Thèse, Université Pierre et Marie Curie - Paris VI)

Rode, F., *Optegnelser fra Finmarken, samlede i aarene 1826-1834.* Skien, 1842.

Scheffer, Johan, *Waarachtige en Aen-merkens-waardige Historie van Lapland.* Amsterdam, 1682. (Latin original 1673)

Serning, Inga, 'Lappbarnen, deras vård och oppfostran i spädbarnsåldern och lekaåldern'. *Norrbotten, Norrbottens läns hembygdsföreningens årsbok* 1949, pp. 55-109.

Thalbitzer, W. (ed.), The Ammassalik eskimo. Contributions to the ethnology of the East Greenland natives'. *Meddelelser om Gronland* 39 (1914) no. 1, pp. 1-755.

About the authors

Drs A. Bant – anthropologist, SNV Netherlands Development Organisation, The Hague, the Netherlands

Dr R.G. Barr – Professor of Pediatrics and Psychiatry, McGill University, Montreal, Canada

M.A. Bolland – honorary staff member, Tropenmuseum, Amsterdam, the Netherlands

P. Bramlage – visual artist, Amsterdam, the Netherlands

M. Brodie – University of Witwatersrand, Johannesburg, South Africa

Drs D.A.P. van Duuren – Documentalist of Collections, Tropenmuseum, Amsterdam, the Netherlands

T. Emelianenko – Russian Museum of Ethnography, St Petersburg, Russia

R. Heringa – The Hague, the Netherlands

Drs E. van der Hoeven – The Hague, the Netherlands

Drs I.C. van Hout – Curator of Textiles, Tropenmuseum, Amsterdam, the Netherlands

Dr E.M. Kloek – historian, University of Utrecht, the Netherlands

M. de Lataillade – Musée de l'Homme (Museum of Mankind), Paris, France

Dr R. de Leeuw – paediatrician, Academic Medical Center, University of Amsterdam, the Netherlands

Drs A.R. Lith – sociologist, Amsterdam, the Netherlands

Dr B. Menzel – anthropologist, Krefeld, Germany

B. Robbe – curator, Musée de l'Homme (Museum of Mankind), Paris, France

Drs D.A.M. Smidt – curator, Rijksmuseum voor Volkenkunde (National Museum of Ethnology), Leiden, the Netherlands

Dr K. Solovieva – Russian Museum of Ethnography, St Petersburg, Russia

A. Tabak – lecturer, Hogeschool voor de Kunsten Utrecht (Utrecht School of the Arts), the Netherlands

Prof. H.L. Whittier, PhD – Michigan State University, USA

Dr P.R. Whittier, PhD – anthropologist, Medical Anthropology Quarterly, USA

Dr N. Zorgdrager – cultural anthropologist, Groningen, the Netherlands

Drs (doctorandus) is a Dutch academic title ranking between a Masters and a PhD.